CULTURE AND EVERYDAY LIFE

DAVID INGLIS

Routledge
Taylor & Francis Group

LONDON AND NEW YORK

First published 2005
by Routledge
2 Park Square, Milton Park, Abingdon, Oxon, OX14 4RN

Simultaneously published in the USA and Canada
by Routledge
270 Madison Ave, New York, NY 10016

Routledge is an imprint of the Taylor & Francis Group

Typeset in Garamond and Scala Sans by Taylor & Francis Books
Printed and bound in Great Britain by MPG Books Ltd, Bodmin

British Library Cataloguing in Publication Data
A catalogue record for this book is available from the British Library

Library of Congress Cataloging-in-Publication Data
A catalog record for this book has been requested

ISBN 0–415–31926–9 (hbk)
ISBN 0–415–31925–0 (pbk)

To J. U.
The greatest of mentors

CONTENTS

SERIES EDITOR'S FOREWORD

'The New Sociology' is a series that takes its cue from massive social transformations currently sweeping the globe. Globalization, new information technologies, the techno-industrialization of warfare and terrorism, the privatization of public resources, the dominance of consumerist values: these developments involve major change to the ways people live their personal and social lives today. Moreover, such developments impact considerably on the tasks of sociology, and the social sciences more generally. Yet, for the most part, the ways in which global institutional transformations are influencing the subject matter and focus of sociology have been discussed only in the more advanced, specialized literature of the discipline. I was prompted to develop this series, therefore, in order to introduce students – as well as general readers who are seeking to come to terms with the practical circumstances of their daily lives – to the various ways in which sociology reflects the transformed conditions and axes of our globalizing world.

Perhaps the central claim of the series is that sociology is fundamentally linked to the practical and moral concerns of everyday life. The authors in this series – examining topics all the way from the body to globalization, from self-identity to consumption – seek to demonstrate the complex, contradictory ways in which sociology is a necessary and very practical aspect of our personal and public lives. From one angle, this may seem uncontroversial. After all, many classical sociological analysts as well as those associated with the classics of social theory emphasized the practical basis of human knowledge, notably Emile Durkheim, Karl Marx, Max Weber, Sigmund Freud and George Simmel, among many others. And yet there are major respects in which the professionalization of academic sociology during the latter period of the twentieth century led to a retreat from the everyday issues and moral basis of sociology itself. (For an excellent discussion of the changing relations between practical and professional sociologies see Charles Lemert, *Sociology After the Crisis*, Second Edition, Boulder, CO: Paradigm, 2004.) As worrying as such a retreat from the practical and moral grounds of the discipline is, one of the main consequences of recent global transformations in the field of sociology has been a renewed emphasis on the mediation of everyday events and experiences by distant social forces, the intermeshing of the local and global in the production of social practices, and on ethics and moral responsibility at both the individual and collective levels. The New Sociology Series traces out these concerns across the terrain of various themes and thematics, situating everyday social practices in the broader context of life in a globalizing world.

In *Culture and Everyday Life*, David Inglis deftly traces the emergence of culture as a specific field of sociological analysis, analysing with great flair the contradictions of the historical and political split between 'culture' and 'society'. This is a most wonderful introduction to the sociology of culture for both the beginning student and teachers in the field, in part because Inglis's great strength lies is his tenacity in pursuing what sociology in particular and social theory in general contribute to a wider appreciation of the dynamics of culture, all of which he contrasts and compares with related fields, most notably the currently fashionable terrain of cultural studies. In the very broadest terms, *Culture and Everyday Life* can be read as an introduction to the sociological analysis of cultural practices and artistic forms – from poetry to Picasso, Marxism to MTV, aesthetics to Americanization or Western imperialism. The word 'culture' thus charts within its historical unfolding, as Inglis powerfully demonstrates, a broader history of sociological thinking in particular and a generalized account of social life as a whole. 'Culture' here means access to certain sociological angles on artistic and aesthetic activity, as represented in the intellectual departures of leading social theorists such as Georg Simmel, Raymond Williams, Stuart Hall and Pierre Bourdieu, amongst many others.

But the book is much more than a definitional mapping of culture from the perspective of sociology. For 'culture', as Inglis rightly notes, is among one of the most complex words in the English language – scooping up as it does ideas and ideologies, everyday practices and lived experience, fine living and pre-packaged lifestyles, lofty high and standardized mass forms, mass and minority cultures. If the sociology of culture can thus be approached in terms of underwriting the power, multiplicity and autonomy of the cultural field itself, it also encodes a number of central sociological issues. These include, as Inglis subtly charts, questions of human agency and social structure, imagination and routinization, the radically new and the force of tradition, interpersonal change and social consensus. Recast in this way, he allows us to grasp the degree to which the relations between cultural discourses and social interests are complex and variable ones – at times seamlessly interwoven and homogenizing, and at other times a matter of contradiction and heterogeneity. A sociological theory of culture has most value, according to Inglis, when it can illuminate the institutional processes by which this doubleness is constituted and reproduced.

Throughout the postmodern 1980s and apolitical 1990s, we have seen a turn within the social sciences and humanities to the notion of culture as never before. Culture became, in effect, a vital preoccupation of the academy as a means of both creatively engaging with new globalizing forms of sociality as well as defensively turning away from various pressing public political issues, from poverty and famine to drugs and debt. On balance, Inglis makes a case for the defence of cultural sociology, thinking that the political gains have outweighed the losses. From the politics of consumerism to resistances of postmodern global culture, a critical sociology of culture has played an important role in revitalizing the political ends of the social sciences. In providing lucid interpretations of the key sociological traditions addressing different definitions of culture, from neo-Marxist and neo-Weberian to post-structuralist, feminist and postmodern theories, Inglis's *Culture and Everyday Life* expertly brings together the various modes of culture that shape, and are shaped by, everyday social life.

Anthony Elliott
Canterbury, 2005

ACKNOWLEDGEMENTS

I would like to thank all of those who were involved in one way or another in the making of this book. I would like to thank Professor Anthony Elliott, for having both the courage to commission me to write it and then the patience to wait for it to appear, while a long stretch of 'everyday life' passed by to become a *longue durée*. In the same vein, I would like to thank Constance Sutherland at Routledge for her input into the production process. At Aberdeen, the intellectual stewpot where the ideas for this book matured, I would particularly like to thank Roland Robertson, Karen O'Reilly, Norman Stockman, Rhoda Wilkie and John Bone, either for suggesting ideas and supplying references or for putting up with someone who, while writing this book, had become more concerned to theorize about everyday life than to go out and just live it.

David Inglis

INTRODUCTION

CULTURE AND THE EVERYDAY

Bob invited me to dinner at his flat one Thursday evening and we made arrangements that he would meet me by car at his local underground station. He cooked an excellent medium-rare steak and french fries, served with a dressed salad and a glass of claret. After our meal we settled in his lounge with the remainder of the wine. I found him to be far too amorous. I turned down his advances and would do no more than kiss him. At the end of the evening he drove me back to the tube (station) and suggested I meet him there the following Thursday, but this time with a pound of sausages as he would have no time for shopping. The next Thursday I arrived at the underground station at the appointed hour but there was no Bob. After waiting forty minutes and not knowing exactly where he lived and still there was no Bob. I went home, taking my sausages with me.

(Smith, 2001: 80–81)

THE BANALITY OF THE EVERYDAY

Nothing seems more transparently obvious than our day-to-day activities. All of us spend our days doing things that are so routine and mundane that it hardly seems worth talking about them – getting up, cleaning our teeth, showering, making a cup of tea or coffee, walking the dog, taking children to school, saying hello to the neighbours, getting on the commuter train, watching daytime TV, taking papers to the photocopying room at work, having a quick lunch, returning home, watching evening TV, having a nightcap, going to bed. All of these sorts of activities plus a million and one other equally banal things are the stuff from which our everyday lives are made.

Even getting stood up on a date, as Sylvia Smith describes above, while slightly out of the ordinary, is still ordinary enough for us all to recognize it as a fairly typical feature of the modern dating scene and thus of everyday existence. Thus in one way Sylvia's story is peculiar to her and her experience of life. After all, we are not all stood up while carrying a pound of sausages. Everyone's everyday life is in certain senses unique to them. But in another way, most people have the same sorts of everyday experiences, making the routines of everyday life 'common' not just in the sense of mundane but also in the sense of shared by most, if not all, people.

If someone was to ask us to describe our daily lives, we might be hard pressed to find anything to talk about that we might say was at all interesting, because daily life suggests routine, and routine by definition involves things that are not out of the ordinary. If pressed to describe what I did yesterday, I might try to find some things that made yesterday a little bit different from other days just like it. I might mention that the bus I get to work was twenty minutes late, leaving me standing in the cold for much longer than I would have liked. Or I might say that I had called my mother and she had told me how an old friend of the family she had met recently was doing. Or again, I might talk about how there had been a little scene at lunchtime, when one colleague had got a touch annoyed by another person's comments about something. If I was pressed further to describe in great detail what I did on a certain day – as sometimes is requested of witnesses in court cases – I would probably in a rather embarrassed way describe when I got out of bed and how grumpy I felt about that, exactly how long it took me to brush my teeth, what type of toothpaste I used, how diligently I brushed, and hundreds of other tiny and apparently wholly insignificant details that I would feel could hardly be of any interest to anybody, not even myself (Sumner, 1961 [1906]).

The point here is that when someone is called to reflect upon and describe their everyday existences, not only is the point of doing that probably somewhat obscure to them but also it is rather difficult to put into words what one takes for granted every single day of one's life. Asking people to reflect upon activities they rarely, if ever, reflect upon can render them unsure as to what to say and how to put into words things that they generally never vocalize. As Anthony Giddens (cited in Tomlinson, 1997: 174) puts it:

> We live day-to-day lives in which for most of what we do we can't give any reason. We dress as we do, we walk around as we do [and do innumerable other everyday things] ... these things are part of a tissue of day-to-day social activity which really isn't explained. It's hard to say why we do these things except that they're there and we do them.

SOCIETY AND THE EVERYDAY

If everyday life is so banal, why would one want to write about it? The answer to that question is: *because everyday life contains within it more significance than we might think.* As Georg Simmel (1950: 413) put the point, 'even the most banal externalities of life' are expressions of the wider social and cultural order.

All human beings have everyday lives – the banal run of everyday experiences is shared by all humans across the planet. But my everyday life as a relatively privileged, white middle-class man will in some ways be rather different from, say, a black working-class woman. While we will both share the same basic routine experiences – waking up, preparing for the day, doing things during the day, eating, sleeping – that woman's version of those experiences may be very different from my own. She may have to rise at five in the morning to go to work; her work may be back-breaking and unrewarding, both mentally and financially. If she fails to get to work on time, she might face all sorts of sanctions, including being sacked.

My everyday routine as a university lecturer, by contrast, means that on days when I am not teaching, I can turn up at the office any time that I please, and if I don't appear at all ('working at home') then no one will be bothered. The worst I can expect is if I arrive, as is usual, at the office sometime in mid- or late morning, a particular colleague more attuned to early morning rises than I will say to me as I enter my room, 'Here comes the nightshift!' And my work is far from being back-breaking, even if it involves the stress of missed publishing deadlines and the fear of boring students rigid in lectures.

The point then is this: different people have different sorts of everyday lives; the sorts of everyday routines and activities they engage in depends on their social position; understanding how everyday life is structured for particular people requires understanding how the society in which they live is itself structured and organized. Quite simply, if we want to understand everyday life thoroughly, beyond seeing it just as an assemblage of dull and unremarkable activities, we have to understand how wider society and social structures make it the way it is for different sorts of people. Conversely, we cannot understand how a society, or a particular part of it, works unless we understand what goes on in everyday life for different groups of people. Sociology is the study of 'society' and 'social relations'. Thus understanding the deeper significances of everyday life requires a sociological comprehension of the social contexts in which different sorts of everyday experiences happen, sociological understanding often seeking to go beyond the level of particular persons' perspectives and perceptions, to get at 'deeper' and more hidden aspects of social structure and organization. On the other hand, just as everyday life can tell us a great deal about society, it follows that the study of everyday life has much to teach the sociologist about how particular societies and specific aspects of those societies operate. Sociology can inform us about everyday life just as everyday life can enrich sociological knowledge, fleshing out general ideas and theories with a wealth of details and specificities.

CULTURE AND THE EVERYDAY

However, it is not enough just to think about the connections between 'society' (and 'social structures', 'social institutions', 'social systems', and so on) on the one side, and everyday activities on the other. No human society can exist without the people within it having certain ideas, values, norms, beliefs and ways of thinking. Another way of saying that is that every society is in part made up of, runs on the basis of and requires 'culture'. Humans, unlike (many but not all) animals, are cultural beings (de Waal, 2002). What I mean is that humans do possess certain basic 'in-built' and thus 'natural' dispositions, like the capacity to communicate through language. But humans are not totally genetically 'hard-wired' to think and act in certain ways. Unlike a lion, for example, which is instinctually predisposed to act out a limited repertoire of behaviours, humans are not as restricted. When a lion sees an animal it regards as prey, it will be disposed to hunt it. Humans, however, do not respond automatically to particular stimuli. How they respond to them depends upon the set of ideas and attitudes − the culture − that they have been socialized into by the society and/or the particular social group they were raised within.

This means that someone brought up in one cultural context could respond to a particular thing or situation in a manner somewhat or indeed very different from someone brought up in another cultural context. In all places around the world where there are lions, they do very much the same sorts of things. Humans too all across the world do the same kinds of things − eat, sleep, defecate, make love and so on. But the *specific ways* in which they do those things, and the manners in which they *think about* those things, vary from one society to another and from one cultural context to another. Sometimes the differences between two contexts may be very small, sometimes they may be very great. In some societies, for example, the culture is such that one can defecate and urinate in public and no one will be bothered very much, but in other societies the 'toilet culture' (i.e. the ideas about how to manage urination and defecation) is such that people are appalled about such activities happening in the public eye. Lions and most other animals are not very bothered about how they void their bodily wastes. Humans, however, can be very bothered about such things; but not all humans are. How a particular group thinks about and does certain things is a function not of instinct but of the culture of the group (Mead, 1938).

The upshot of all this for the understanding of everyday life is that it is not just the social position of a person that structures their everyday activities but the cultural conditions they operate within too. The cultural conditions each person works within are, in complex modern societies, multiple and overlapping. At the most general level, we can talk about ideas, notions, dispositions and ways of thinking and feeling that are pervasive throughout all Western societies (e.g. an emphasis on the importance and autonomy of the individual). We can also investigate how people's activities are related to national and regional cultures (e.g. how Protestant ideas continue to be present, albeit perhaps in disguised forms, in Scandinavia just as Catholic attitudes still pertain in many parts of Southern Europe). At a more concrete level, we can look at how being part of a social class, an ethnic group, a professional grouping and other sorts of social belonging and affiliation can have ramifications for how people operate in their everyday affairs, as each of these sorts of social collectivity has identifiable cultural traits. This would also be the case for different sorts of jobs and occupations, as each of these can have attached to it particular sets of attitudes, expectations and norms. Finally, at the most specific level, we could examine the ways in which the 'cultures' of particular cities and towns, communities and neighbourhoods, places and spaces can help to create what a person experiences as their daily business. For all of these levels of 'culture', we would have to see how they intersected with 'society', with the social structures and institutions which can have such a great effect on how everyday affairs are lived.

THINKING 'CULTURE'

As this book is about how 'culture' in its various manifestations impinges upon everyday life, we need to be clear from the outset what is meant by 'culture' and how it might be thought about. As almost everyone who has ever written anything about culture has observed, it can mean a lot of things, some of which complement each other and some of which do not. In the early 1950s, for example, the American anthropologists Alfred Kroeber and Clyde Kluckhohn (1963 [1952]) undertook a review of all the diverse meanings of 'culture' in the available literature, and what they understood as its close conceptual relative 'civilization'. They found 164 separate definitions of what the word 'culture' could refer to.

In the same vein, the literary scholar Raymond Williams (1976) noted in a well-known passage that 'culture' was one of the most complicated words in the English language, in that it possessed a wide range of meanings that had mutated a lot over time. The main meanings of 'culture' he identified as predominant in the present day were:

1) 'high culture', a meaning related to the words 'art' and 'civilization';
2) personal refinement; such as when we talk of a 'cultured person';
3) cultural objects and products such as books, films, and TV shows;
4) the 'whole way of life' of a given group of people; such as when we

say 'working class culture' or 'Japanese culture'. This meaning involves defining 'culture' as all the ways of thinking, understanding, feeling, believing and acting 'characteristic' of a particular group (and thus *not* characteristic of another group). Such dispositions have been learned, 'socialised' (or 'enculturated') into an individual by being reared within the parameters of the group.

Therefore 'culture' can refer to either 'high culture' or 'popular culture'; the ways of thinking and feeling characteristic of everyone in a given group or society, or the capacities of individuals; the attitudes and habits of the many or of the few. In sum, 'culture' is a word that has a lot of work to do in the English language, because it is used to describe so many different things. This can lead to great confusion. Such a situation demands that when we talk about 'culture' we make clear exactly what meaning of it we have in mind. I will endeavour to do this throughout this book.

In other work (Inglis and Hughson, 2003), I have set out what I take to be the most general aspects of 'culture' conceived in Williams's fourth and most generic definition of it, namely as the 'whole way of life' of a given group of people. Those aspects are very relevant to this book, given its focus on cultural currents in everyday life, and so here they are (in a slightly expanded form):

1   *Culture comprises the patterns of ideas, values and beliefs common to a particular group of people, their 'characteristic' ways of thinking and feeling.*
    It does not matter whether the group is small or large, or whether it comprises a set of people within a particular 'society', or everyone within that society, or people from different societies related to each other in some way across 'national' boundaries. Culture is defined as being part of the collective life of given groups of human beings.

    Culture comprises recurring patterns of ideas, values and beliefs. A 'culture' persists to some extent over time. It has some capacities to endure over time, as well as to change and be changed.
2   *The culture of one group differentiates it from other groups, each of which has its 'own' culture.*
    Different types of group can be said to have 'their own' cultures: the culture of a 'nation' (e.g. German culture, Irish culture), of a social class (e.g. working-class culture, upper middle-class culture), of an

ethnic group within a nation (e.g. Mexican–American culture), of a group outside the 'mainstream' culture (e.g. a youth subculture of punks, a 'criminal' subculture). Each of these types of group can be said to have its own culture, its own distinctive (or relatively distinctive) set of ideas, values and beliefs.

This is not, though, to claim that there are no overlaps between 'different' cultures, and no elements that they might share (e.g. working-class culture in the United States is part of, and shares many of the features of, more general 'American' culture).

3   *Culture contains meanings. Culture is meaningful.*

These meanings are the ways through which people in the group understand, make sense of, and respond intellectually and emotionally to, the world around them.

This aspect of culture has been particularly stressed by those thinkers who have been influenced by the ideas of the philosopher Immanuel Kant, the Kantian tradition being perhaps the mainstream way of thinking about culture in the social sciences. It is a Kantian approach that animates Durkheim's view that a particular culture is made up of a set of collective representations (Durkheim and Mauss, 1969 [1903]). A particularly important set of classifications that Durkheim (2001 [1912]) identified were the ways in which each particular culture classifies things into two categories, the 'sacred' on the one hand (things that are seen to be 'holy', special and literally extraordinary) and the 'profane' (the opposite of sacred things, things that are defined as everyday, routine and ordinary) on the other.

While all cultures according to Durkheim divide things in the world up in this way, each culture has its own distinctive understanding of what fits into each category. What is regarded as 'special' in one cultural context could be regarded as not at all special in another, and vice versa. This leads to the conclusion that there is some variance among different groups of people, living at different times and in different places, as to what counts as part of 'profane' everyday life, which is the opposite of 'sacred' special occasions. As Alvin Gouldner (1975) notes, different societies have had somewhat different ideas as to what counts as 'everyday life'. However, all of them presumably define the 'everyday' as involving things that happen on a day-to-day basis and that are not especially marked out and defined as somehow 'out of the ordinary'.

Also in a Kantian vein, Max Weber (cited in Turner, 1996: 5) defined culture as 'a finite segment of the meaningless infinity of the world process, a segment on which human beings confer meaning and significance'. Both Weber and Durkheim are saying much the same thing in different ways: the culture of a group makes sense of the world for people in a particular group; it is the framework through which they experience and understand the world around them. Humans therefore can be seen as having no direct access to 'reality'; instead, their reality is thoroughly shaped by culture (Berger and Luckmann, 1967), especially through the means of the categories of the particular language they use. Culture and language are closely connected, if not synonymous; the way a language 'carves up' reality and endows it with meaning profoundly shapes the ways people who use that language understand things (Saussure, 1959 [1906–1911]).

4 *The ideas, values and beliefs of a group are profoundly implicated in motivating people to act in certain ways.*
Max Weber's definition of sociology was 'the interpretive understanding of social action' (cited in Alexander, 1983: 30). What this means is that sociology is concerned with how certain values, ideas and beliefs – that is, cultural forms – motivate people to act in the ways that they do. Functionalist sociology, at its most sophisticated in the work of Talcott Parsons (1961), looks not only at the culturally motivated nature of people's activities, but also at how larger-scale social systems require people to act in certain ways and how such systems motivate individuals to act in those ways. As Parsons (1961: 963) puts it, 'the structure of cultural meanings constitutes the "ground" of any system of action'. That is to say, culture is made up of more general values, which generate specific norms, which in turn guide people to act in ways congruent with the 'needs' of the wider social structures in which they operate.

5 *The ideas, values and beliefs of a group are embodied in symbols and artefacts.*
These symbols can be pictorial or can be part of a written language.

These artefacts are physical objects which are imprinted in some way with the ideas, values and beliefs of the group.

6 *Culture is learned.*
Culture is transmitted by one generation of people to the next generation.

This learning process means that individuals internalize the ideas, values and beliefs of the group. These become habitual and taken for granted, and are generally experienced as 'natural' rather than learned. This raises the issue of culturally shaped 'life-worlds' which we will examine below.

7 *Culture is arbitrary.*
Culture is the result primarily of human activities, rather than wholly the product of 'nature'. It is neither totally 'natural' nor inevitably the way it happens to be. It could be somewhat different from the way it is, if the life conditions of the group change.

8 *Culture and forms of social power are intimately bound up with each other.*
An influential stream of thought within sociology that includes both Marxism and Weberianism sees culture as always being shaped and influenced in one way or another by powerful institutions and groups in society, whether individuals in those groups are fully aware of this or not. For Karl Marx (in McLellan, 1984: 184), the dominant culture in a society is associated with and generated by the ruling class(es) in that society: 'The ideas of the ruling class are in every epoch the ruling ideas: i.e. the class which is the ruling material force of society, is at the same time its ruling intellectual force.' Culture on this view is synonymous with ideology. It helps to reproduce the power of dominant classes by defining reality in ways that suit their interests. For Weber, while culture is not fully reducible to forms of social power, it is closely connected to them (Collins, 1986). For Michel Foucault (1981), different languages ('discourses') not only define the world in certain ways, but define it in ways that serve the interests and reflect the power of certain groups: for example, the language used by psychologists to define and deal with mental patients acts as a form of control over the latter.

While the identification of most of these aspects is I think relatively uncontroversial, issues in points 1 and 7 contain some knotty issues. In the first place and as we will see more in Chapter 4, 'globalization' challenges us to consider how 'culture' can still be the 'possession' of a specific group of people when people in that group could be scattered across the globe and not contained within particular geographical areas. In the second place, while it is social scientific orthodoxy to claim that 'culture' and 'nature' are wholly distinct entities, some people – of which I am one – do not agree with this. This is an issue that will be bracketed off throughout most of the book, and in Chapter 1 we will consider some of the ways in which 'culture' is indeed 'above', 'beyond' and irreducible to 'nature'. However I will return to this vexed issue in the overall conclusion.

Despite these complications, a shorthand characterization of 'culture' would see as it involving *what different groups of people believe, think and feel*.

DEFAMILIARIZING THE FAMILIAR

How might we go about examining the ways in which cultural forces, together with social factors, influence, shape and structure our everyday activities? A key aspect of both sociological and anthropological responses to this question is to emphasize that one must take what is routine and very familiar to one, and try to defamiliarize oneself with it, making it seem strange and peculiar, rather than ordinary and banal.

We might usefully call the everyday circumstances in which we live the 'life-world'. This was a term coined by the phenomenological philosopher Edmund Husserl towards the beginning of the twentieth century. By it Husserl (1970: 380–381) meant 'the always taken-for-granted ... the world that is constantly pre-given ... the world of which we are all conscious in life as the world of us all'. What he meant by this was that human life can only function if the individual person has a certain sense of stability and certainty as to the world around them. We need routines and habits in order for us to function, because if everything in the world about us kept coming as a surprise to us, as totally novel and unprecedented, we would have no bearings in life, we would be totally dazed and confused (Sumner, 1961 [1906]: 1037). To use more modern terminology, the individual needs a certain sense of psychological security, to the effect that the world around him or her is relatively predictable and understandable and is not just totally chaotic

(Giddens, 1991). We need a sense of routine and stability in our every-day lives. That sense, for each person, is their life-world, their perception and experience of the orderliness and relative stability of the world around them.

However, we cannot just talk about each single person's life-world. Life-worlds are also shared; they involve expectations and ideas about, and orientations towards, the worlds that are shared by the members of a particular group. These groups could be akin to the ones mentioned above – nations, classes, ethnic groups and so on. In other words, the life-world for each group is shaped by the culture of the group. The life-world of a person is made up of all the intersecting cultural forces of the various different groups they belong to, and is structured by the social contexts they operate within.

The central characteristic of any life-world is its pre-reflective, taken-for-granted nature. People exist for the most part in their life-world like fish in water. So 'natural' does the life-world seem for each person that they do not generally experience it as anything other than just 'the way things are'. It is only in certain situations that one can be forced out of one's life-world, where all one's routine expectations about life crumble (e.g. when a 'respectable' citizen is arrested by the police for a serious crime, a situation such a person can find incredibly traumatic, all their usual routines and ways of thinking are disrupted and challenged). As the life-world is shaped by cultural forces, but these are generally not experienced as anything but 'natural', we can say that we exist 'in culture' but we are generally not aware of that fact. Thus when we are defamiliarizing ourselves with our everyday routines, what we are doing is, as it were, 'escaping' from the life-world and coming to look at it 'from the outside', as if it were foreign to us. We come to see the oddities and peculiarities of our life-world, as if we were looking at the thoughts and activities of a group of people who live in ways very alien to us. Just as other people's 'culture' often seems very odd to us, defamiliarization means coming to see our own life-world, which we generally never realize is anything other than 'natural', as not 'natural at *all*' – it is but one way of thinking and acting among a whole series of possible other ways.

Defamiliarizing one's own life-world can be more difficult than investigating the nature and contours of someone else's, because it is generally easier to spot the oddities and specificities of another person's way of life than one's own. Looking at the life-worlds of people who lived in the past is a good way of seeing how cultural forces that they themselves were generally unaware of shaped their everyday attitudes and routines. Here for example is an entry from the journal of the English diarist Samuel Pepys (2003: 87–88), dated Saturday, 20 October 1660:

> This morning [some]one came to me to advise with me where to make me a window into my cellar in lieu of one which ... had [been] stopped up, and going down into my cellar to look I stepped into a great heap of turds by which I found that Mr. Turner's house of office [i.e. toilet] is full and comes into my cellar, which do trouble me, but I shall have it helped. To my Lord's [the Earl of Sandwich, Pepys's former employer] by land, calling at several places about business, where I dined with my Lord and Lady; when he was very merry, and did talk very high how he would have a French cook, and a master of his horse ... among other things, my Lady saying that she could get a good merchant for her daughter Jem., he answered, that he would rather see her with a pedlar's pack at her back, so she married a gentleman, than she should marry a citizen. This afternoon, going through London, and calling at Crowe's the upholster's, in Saint Bartholomew's, I saw the limbs of some of our new traitors set upon Aldersgate, which was a sad sight to see; and a bloody week this and the last have been, there being ten hanged, drawn, and quartered. Home, and after writing a letter to my uncle by the post, I went to bed.

For Pepys, writing in the latter half of the seventeenth century, all the things he describes were part of his everyday routine and quite 'normal'. But for us, living within different life-worlds, centred around somewhat different expectations and attitudes, we can spot the specific cultural forces that shaped Pepys's everyday routines. On that particular Saturday, Pepys found that his neighbour's toilet facilities had spilled into his cellar. Pepys lived more than 200 years before water-flushed toilets became the norm in England, so he has rather different attitudes to finding a great pile of turds in his basement than you or I might today; people then were much more sanguine about such matters, whereas today we have become much more intensely disgusted by human wastes (Inglis, 2001). Pepys's life-world was such that while he did say that the mess 'do trouble me', he could go on to note with a shrug that 'I shall have it helped', by getting workmen to come and fix the problem. A modern diarist, living in a cultural situation of much greater intolerance of such matters, would likely not have responded to the situation in such a matter-of-fact way as described here.

Other things can strike us as rather peculiar about the events of Pepys's Saturday, and the attitudes that underpinned it. The routine talk about servants seems odd in a present-day context where widespread use of domestic servants has all but disappeared (with nannies and childminders and suchlike no longer regarded as servants but redefined as service sector employees). The snobbery of the Earl of Sandwich as to whom his daughter should marry – a bona fide 'gentleman' rather than a mere bourgeois 'citizen' – also strikes us as peculiar in these apparently more egalitarian times of ours. In the same vein, while Pepys records that there have been quite a lot of public executions recently, he does not think that seeing the corpses of those who have been hung, drawn and quartered in the middle of London is very out of the ordinary. In a world like our own, where death is generally hidden away behind the professional screens of the medic, the mortician and the undertaker, such a sight would involve great unease and disgust, as well as possibly outrage about the nature of executions carried out by the government. But all of these things were quite normal in the life-world of Samuel Pepys, a condition he lived within without being reflectively aware of it, just as today we do not generally experience our existences within culturally and socially shaped contexts as anything other than the normal routine of life.

Exploring the ways in which culture shapes our own life-world is often difficult but certainly not impossible. A nice example of doing just that is given by the French writer Georges Perec when, sitting at a corner café in the centre of Paris, he commands himself to 'describe the number of operations the driver of a vehicle is subjected to when he parks merely in order to go and buy a hundred grams of fruit jelly'. Perec (1997 [1974]: 51–52) describes the rigmarole the driver goes through in this way:

- parks by means of a certain amount of toing and froing
- switches off the engine
- withdraws the key, setting off a first anti-theft device

- extricates himself from the vehicle
- winds up the left-hand front window
- locks it
- checks that the left-hand rear door is locked;
- if not:
- opens it
- raises the handle inside
- slams the door
- checks it's locked securely
- circles the car; if need be, checks that the boot is locked properly
- checks that the right-hand rear door is locked; if not, recommences the sequence of operations already carried out on the left-hand rear door
- winds up the right-hand front window
- shuts the right-hand front door
- locks it
- before walking away, looks all around him as if to make sure the car is still there and that no-one will come and take it away.

Perec's intention is characteristic of what one must do in order to defamiliarize the taken-for-granted contours of the life-world. He wants to gaze so hard at the 'ordinary' that it stops being ordinary and starts to seem peculiar, even to the point of seeming rather extraordinary. It might seem the most natural thing in the world to park one's car, but the life-world of the motorist is underpinned by all sorts of cultural assumptions, which nonetheless rarely come to light in practice. After all, the car is a relatively new invention and people have invented ways of living in and with it (Urry, 2004); but these inventions come over time to seem just 'normal' and unremarkable. But if a Martian were taking notes about how people in Western societies use cars, he, she or it would take back home the knowledge that, for example, cars are an important part of social status, one's car is often a source of great pride, that entering a car can turn even the most mild-mannered person into an aggressive demon, and that cars often have little rituals attached to them, as in Perec's example of the complicated series of manoeuvres he observed in the art of parking.

A touch of wry humour can be observed in his description towards the end, where the driver is seen to turn round to check if his car is still where he left it a second before. I have seen this in the street a thousand times, but it was only reading Perec's description that made me aware of how odd, if you examine it with the eyes of a stranger, such a small and otherwise unremarkable behaviour can seem. Turning to see if the car is 'all right' is perhaps associated with pride in ownership or fear of reprimand from the traffic authorities. If the former, then the behaviour is connected to the pride in material objects that predominates in a highly consumerist society; if the latter, then it is connected to a characteristic aspect of the culture of social modernity, namely the bureaucratization of everyday life. The life-world of car culture will be further considered in Chapter 2. Meanwhile, what we can say is that defamiliarizing what you see every day allows you not only to discern wider cultural forces at work, but also sometimes to spot the unintentional humour that inheres in everyday life, a humour that only reveals itself when you stand back and look at things with an attitude that has broken with the taken-for-grantedness of the life-world.

APPROACHING CULTURE AND THE EVERYDAY

How do we get access to *'culture' in the 'everyday'* and the *'everyday' aspects of 'culture'*? Raymond Williams (1980 [1961]: 66) gives us a useful start in this direction. He defines culture as possessing three interrelated levels:

> There is the *lived culture* of a particular time and place, only fully accessible to those living in that time and place. There is the *recorded culture*, of every kind, from art to the most everyday facts: the culture of a period. There is also, as the factor connecting lived culture and period cultures, the *culture of the selective tradition.* [My italics]

The *lived culture* is made up of the ways in which a group or groups of people thought and felt at a particular time and place. As Williams says, in a certain way only those who were or are part of the group can know fully what it was like to live in that way (although the notion of 'life-world' suggests that people tend more just to exist 'inside' the lived culture than to think reflectively about it). How then can outsiders know about that lived culture?

Williams's other two levels of culture can help us in that regard. In the first place, the *culture of the selective tradition* is what is conventionally known as 'high culture', the 'art' and 'great works' that (certain) people in a certain context have defined as being somehow more 'special' than and superior to other forms of culture. In modern Western societies, this set includes works by the likes of Shakespeare and Picasso, the creative works that are regarded as being the best of their type. It is possible to see represented or imprinted in these some of the *lived culture* of the time and place in which they were created: Shakespeare's plays can be seen in a way as records of the customs, attitudes and ways of life in Elizabethan England (Lowenthal, 1957). We can get some sort of access to the lived culture – although obviously in a very indirect and possibly very distorted fashion – through the 'art' of that time and place.

The *recorded culture* of a group living at a particular time and place also allows some access to the lived culture. It encompasses all the things that record in some way how people thought and felt, not just 'artworks' but everything from newspapers, films and other mass media products like posters and adverts, to bureaucratic records and official papers, to more intimate documents like personal diaries and written reminiscences. These two can give us an indirect insight into the lived culture, although obviously we have to be on our guard against thinking either that what we read or view necessarily must represent what it purports to represent or indeed if it 'represents' anything at all (Plummer, 2001). The best we can do is be sceptical about what people and records say, and never fully assume that a written or other record of an everyday event totally captures what a particular event was like. Any recollection of an event is both partial and created by a person with a particular way of looking at and judging things, a way of looking that is partly personal to them and partly a product of their 'culture'. For the sake of argument, when in this book I give examples of everyday events recalled and represented by particular people, I will assume that they are generally 'true' or that there is a kernel of truth in them, but of course we must be aware that they are always created from a particular partial perspective and for particular purposes. 'Everyday events' cannot be comprehensively captured and set down on paper; but what we can do is get sideways glimpses of them, partial and limited perspectives of their overall complexity and abundance.

There are other means of investigating culture and the everyday than looking at 'high' and 'recorded' culture, if one is dealing with people alive in the present. Such methods include observation, participant observation and ethnography, all of which have benefits and drawbacks (Bryman, 2001). It would be a mistake to think that any of them can provide us with totally unproblematic and unmediated knowledge of everyday life and the place(s) of culture within it. As Pierre Bourdieu (1990: 150–155) notes, how we construct sociological understandings of people 'out there' in the 'real world', the ways in which we comprehend their mundane existences, are always bound up with both our own personal dispositions and the politics of academic life. Our class, ethnicity, gender and other forms of background can impact on how we talk about and evaluate others. Moreover, how academics represent other people also hinges on what uses they make of that knowledge in the university setting and how they want other academics to understand and respond to that knowledge – do I want to be seen as an 'intellectual' who knows more about 'ordinary people' (itself a loaded term) than they do themselves, or do I want to be regarded as a 'people's champion', standing up for the 'little man' (and woman)? Both perspectives are ideologically loaded. We have therefore to be very attuned to how our own constructions of 'everyday life' and 'culture' reflect our own biases, likes and dislikes, and attitudes.

In saying that, we nonetheless have to find workable means of conceptualizing, investigating and indeed imagining culture in everyday contexts. In this book I have written in a relatively eclectic manner, taking inspiration from, and trying to develop a little, certain established sociological ways of thinking vis-à-vis the main theme (for some classic sociological accounts of everyday life, see Truzzi, 1968). My choice inevitably reflects my own interests and knowledge. In no way is this book intended as a totally comprehensive study of its central theme. It does not fully deal with topics either that I think have been very well covered elsewhere (e.g. consumer behaviours) or on which I am not qualified enough to write upon (e.g. everyday cultures of ethnicity, although I do deal with the 'hybridization' of cultures in Chapter 4). It is rather a series of 'sketches' that, to shift rather inelegantly from a painterly to a musical metaphor, 'riff' upon and explore a number of sociological ways of understanding particular socio-cultural contexts that are (conceivable as) 'everyday' in nature.

A point I would like to stress is that sociology is generally in the business of stereotyping people. For the most part this is a very necessary and useful exercise – we need to draw generalizations about people so we can see general trends and not just stick at the level of particularities. We need to be able to see the wood, not just the particular trees. But it is absolutely crucial to remember, especially when studying 'everyday life', that each person's life is both expressive of wider social and cultural forces *and* specific and unique to them. No one had *exactly* the same experience of fending off an over-amorous suitor and then being stood up on a date as Sylvia Smith, but she shares the experience of other women in similar – but not exactly similar – circumstances. Although she lived an avowedly 'ordinary' life – working as a temp in offices, living all her life in rented accommodation – Sylvia's memoirs show that, like the rest of us, her life was both very mundane and, because it was not exactly like anyone else's, in certain ways and from certain angles, extraordinary too. It is important to avoid a situation whereby sociology in general, and the sociology of culture in particular, cannot see the trees for the wood.

PLAN OF THE BOOK

This book has a relatively simple structure. It is meant to build up a series of connected ways into the sometimes thorny issues attendant upon thinking about how cultural phenomena operate in certain 'everyday' contexts.

In Chapter 1, I present some of the ways in which one can say that far from being fully determined by 'biological' factors, the everyday practices of the human body are profoundly influenced by cultural phenomena.

In Chapter 2, I look at how specifically 'modern' (and 'late modern' and 'post-modern') cultural forces can be said to impact upon, and inhere within, everyday activities.

In Chapter 3, I consider the differences between 'high', 'popular' and 'low' cultures and what sorts of mundane activities happen within, and are influenced by, these different 'levels' of culture.

In Chapter 4, I examine the ways in which the forces associated with 'globalization' may be altering the cultural fabric of everyday life.

In the overall conclusion, I suggest some ways in which the sociological study of the cultural elements of everyday life might progress in
the future.

1

CULTURE, 'NATURE' AND EVERYDAY LIFE

INTRODUCTION

It is a very obvious point, but everyday life would be impossible for each of us if we did not have bodies. It is through the means of the body that we do the things that we do on an everyday basis. The body both constricts and prevents certain things but also allows us to do other things. Certain tasks and activities are more, or less, achievable depending not on what *type* of body you have or are seen by others to have. If you are regarded by others as 'beautiful', then you will probably have less difficulty than a less 'beautiful' person in finding what you might take to be an equally 'attractive' partner. Those deemed less lovely than you who want an attractive partner will have to achieve that through other means, such as through power, money or social standing (Etcoff, 2000). Yet what counts as 'beautiful' in one cultural context can be very different from what pertains in another. Human ideals of what counts as sexually attractive are not fully determined by biology; we are not fully pre-programmed to find certain sorts of people sexually appealing or not. This shows that how one's body is perceived by others is to a large extent – and some claim totally – a matter of culture, and how one's body shape and look are culturally defined can have large ramifications as to how one operates on a day-to-day basis, achieving or not achieving one's routine aims (achieving a certain 'look', being thought attractive, getting sex, and so on). Cultural forces are at work in how one uses one's body, how that body 'feels' to one, and how others respond to one by responding to one's body. The body, therefore, can be seen as much as a cultural phenomenon as a biological one.

In this chapter, I will look at a number of different ways in which we can think about the relationships between 'nature' on the one hand and 'culture' on the other. I will examine this issue in terms of how the latter impacts upon the former in the form of the human body when it is engaged in the course of its everyday activities. I will do this by examining the role cultural forces play in the organization and management of human bodies in everyday contexts. I will first look at a view that claims that 'culture' plays a key role in human life, in that it works to 'tame' natural human instincts, bringing them into line with the needs of particular forms of social organization. I will then look at such issues in light of how defecation and urination are culturally organized by particular 'toilet cultures'. Then I move on to examine how it can be argued that cultural forces profoundly shape the ways in which our bodies move and act. I will look at this issue in terms of how bodies are shaped by norms associated with gender and with social class. In these various ways, I will illustrate the main point of this chapter: humans are 'cultural' as much as 'biological' beings, and this fact has profound ramifications for how we live our everyday lives.

'CULTURE' AGAINST 'NATURE'

Cultural forces – ideas, attitudes and symbols – can be regarded as having a key role to play in human life. They make social organization possible by 'taming' an unruly and undisciplined human nature, in the form of volatile sexual and excretory drives. On this view – and I want to stress that it is just one view, not gospel truth (for criticisms see Foucault, 1981) – human nature is anarchic and unruly. Left to our own devices, without the guiding constraints of culture, each of us would run riot. We would seek immediate gratification of our more basic biological impulses. That means that we might seek out any and every sexual partner we could find. When we got angry about something – for example, if one of our intended sexual partners turned us down – we would be moved to violence, and would take out our anger on the person who stimulated it or on others nearby. Without any form of restraint, we would also immediately gratify ourselves by, for example, defecating and urinating wherever we pleased, regardless of the effects on other people. But by regulating and controlling these otherwise unpredictable and possibly violently emotional drives, culture works to ensure that everyday life is possible, by allowing for regularity, predictability and order. Without the ordering impulses of culture, human life truly would be 'nasty, brutish and short'.

One of the most famous proponents of this sort of view was Sigmund Freud. The word he used to describe the cultural norms and values that restrain our volatile sexual and excretory natures was 'civilization'. On Freud's (1957: 63) view, 'civilization' relies on a 'renunciation of instinctual gratifications ... [and] urgencies'. In other words, cultural norms and values make humans give up their natural dispositions towards promiscuous sex, unregulated defecation and urination, and random acts of violence. One powerful way they make us do this is by imbuing in us a sense of *shame*. 'Civilization' instils in us ways of thinking that make us feel ashamed about doing certain things, such as indulging the sexual drives of our bodies or defecating wherever and whenever. Because we feel ashamed and embarrassed about such things, we are much less likely to engage in unregulated defecation or promiscuous sex, and to use violence to gain sexual partners, than if we had been left to our own devices. In this way, 'civilization' (what people today would call 'culture') comes to have control over us, because it has successfully imbued us with a *moral* sense as to what is right and wrong. The presence of 'civilization' is felt in each and every one of us each time we *refrain* from using violence on other people, or when we feel *ashamed* to be having sexual thoughts about someone, or when we get embarrassed by toiletry matters.

For Freud, each person's psychology is torn between two opposing forces. On the one hand, there is the *id*, the part of the mind under the sway of violent sexual and excretory desires. On the other side is the *superego*, the part of the mind that contains moral ideas. These have been implanted by culture, in order to combat the dark forces of the *id*. In the middle, caught between these two opposing sides, is the *ego*, the person's conscious self. The *ego* is constantly faced with a dilemma: either to obey the dictates of the *id* and to gratify oneself in sexual, excretory and often violent terms, or to obey the culturally induced moral imperatives of the *superego*, which demand that one not indulge oneself in this way. Caught every day between fulfilling our desires or renouncing them, revelling in our more 'animal' side or feeling ashamed and disgusted with it, it is as if each of us has a little angel on one shoulder and a little devil on the other, each constantly whispering into our ears completely contradictory forms of advice. While the 'devil' of 'biological nature' wants us to do whatever we like, no matter how bad the consequences may be for ourselves or for other people, the 'angel' of 'culture' says that we will only be worthy of respect, both from ourselves and from others, and indeed only be truly 'human' rather than a mere animal, if we forego what we instinctively want to do.

Freud's views allow us to see how recurringly in certain everyday situations, certain things that we might want to do can come into contradiction with cultural norms and values, causing in us unease, ambivalence and a certain sense of shame. For example, one might have a great desire to have sex with an attractive person one has just met. But in wanting this one may well come up against a whole series of obstacles, as we saw Sylvia Smith's would-be suitor did in the Introduction to this book. First, the other person may not want to sleep with you; and one reason for that is that they are working within a cultural framework that defines you as not particularly 'attractive'. Second, let us assume that the people we are talking about are on a first date. In most cultures, one is generally expected to engage in some sort of courtship ritual to get sexual consent to sleep with someone. Dating in modern Western societies has certain norms and rules about it – endlessly elaborated and discussed in special guidebooks on the subject – just as much as do the courtship rituals of other societies, for example where arranged marriages are normal. One of the people in our imaginary date might very much want to get together sexually straight away, but the other person might be thinking, on the basis of wider cultural definitions of 'good' and 'bad' behaviour, that sleeping together after a first date is somehow 'wrong'. In heterosexual relationships, women in particular in a society like ours may feel pressure not to submit to the man's advances too early in the courtship process because such behaviour is commonly defined as 'slutty'. Even if both partners find each other incredibly alluring, they both have to deal with certain norms as to how far to go so early in their putative relationship. Both may feel embarrassed and uncertain about how far to give into what they want to do, driven by the biological urge to procreate, and how far to restrain that urge, because they do not want to be seen to be too 'crude' or 'fresh', or 'too easy'.

The Freudian point here would be that these feelings have not just appeared out of the blue, neither are they specific to particular individuals (although some individuals might be more neurotic about such things than others). Rather, such feelings have come from people being brought up in a cultural context which in certain ways 'taboos' sexual thoughts and feelings, and thus makes people uneasy about their sexual desires and the means of fulfilling them. On this view, everyday life is a minefield of possible sexual faux pas, where one can be (seen to be) either too sexually aggressive or too timid; but it is only so because 'natural' biological urges have been culturally defined as 'problems'. Freud argues that any kind of social life requires the cultural taming of 'instinctual' urges; but he also recognized the very ambivalent effects that certain sorts of cultural regulation can have on how people feel about themselves and their own bodies.

TOILET CULTURE

It is not only sex that comes to be culturally regulated in human society but the excretion of bodily wastes too. Humans must eat to live and then must excrete that which has been digested. Without the influence of cultural norms, defecation and urination among adults would presumably occur in the manner of very young children – one would void one's wastes as and when the desire took one. All societies regulate excretion, inculcating their 'toiletry culture' into infants (Inglis, 2001). Children *learn* to be disgusted by turds, they do not just 'naturally' recoil from them. If a response to something is learned, then it is being shaped by a cultural norm, not just by 'nature'.

I agree with Freud that modern Western societies have a particularly strict toiletry culture, which in comparison with other societies is exceptionally oriented around both disgust towards defecatory materials and stern rules as to the proper conduct of oneself in this regard: only certain times and specific places are defined as being legitimate for excretory purposes. As Elias (1995: 443) describes it, both sexual and defecatory matters were throughout early modernity (i.e. from the sixteenth to eighteenth centuries) 'progressively thrust behind the scenes of men's [*sic*] communal social life and invested with feelings of shame ... the regulation of the whole instinctual and affective life by steady self-control becomes more and more stable, more even and more all-embracing'. In other words as modern Western society developed, people became increasingly disgusted with the sexual and defecatory aspects of their bodies, and they felt ever greater needs to cover up these embarrassing features of their corporeal life.

One specific aspect of the strict toiletry norms of Western modernity can be seen in the fact that the norms of capitalist work culture are strongly opposed to workers wasting time at work when there are profits to be made; on this view, 'time is money' (Thompson, 1967). As Hans-Willy Hohn (cited in Adam, 1994: 113) notes, from the eighteenth century onwards,

> work and time are 'cleansed' of orientations and meanings which are antithetical to ... capitalist work-discipline. In the process of industrialisation the cycles of work and relaxation, which formerly accompanied nature and task-bound rhythms, attain their own metric dynamic and gradually become indifferent towards traditional contexts of meaning and significance.

In other words, the capitalistically organized workplace is centred around a search for profit, and workers' bodies are controlled accordingly. It does not matter if the 'natural' rhythms of their bodies – such as needing to go to the toilet – do not fit with the required tempo of work, because the body must keep working in the pursuit of profit, no matter what. As a result, time regimes which could be very different from those of the body 'itself' are imposed upon workers by management. For example, Huw Beynon's (1973: 135) study of the Ford car plant at Halewood near Liverpool contains a passage where an interviewee remarks upon how management imposed a very strict routine on the workers:

> They expect you to work the 480 minutes of the eight hours you're on the clock. They've agreed to have a built-in allowance of *six minutes* for going to the toilet, blowing your nose and that. It takes you six minutes to get your trousers down. (Italics in original)

Here we see in vivid detail one way in which cultural norms – in this case, explicitly thought-out and 'instrumentally rational' ones (see Chapter 2) – impose themselves, or are imposed by specific social contexts, upon bodies. The ways in which those bodies would otherwise have operated if left 'to their own devices' can be very different from the practices expected by cultural norms. The general point here is that in certain everyday social contexts there may be a certain amount of antagonism between cultural expectations and bodily capacities and desires.

We have already seen that the ways in which we think about defecation come in no small part from 'cultural' rather than 'natural' factors. It is also worth mentioning that our thinking about human wastes comes from factors other than concerns about 'hygiene' (Inglis, 2001). Modern medicine rightly shows that human faeces are a ripe source of disease transmission. Thus we flush wastes down the toilet in order to get rid of them, such that they may not transmit or breed germs in our homes. But there is more to our understandings of the dangers of faeces than their hygienic aspects alone. Faeces are also *symbols* for us of what is most offensive, disgusting and low. It is part of our culture that to call someone a 'shit' or a 'turd' is to insult them. There is probably no reason in 'nature' why the objects these words refer to should figure as great sources of insult. But faeces figure as ways of insulting people because modern toiletry culture *defines* them as being filthy (Inglis and Holmes, 2002). Thus it is only because a certain cultural context has decreed that we see faeces as particularly 'dirty' that we do indeed see them that way.

Another interesting way of showing how there are 'cultural' as well as medical–hygienic reasons for us thinking that faeces are filthy and disgusting is this. Great emphasis is put by the makers of toilet paper on how the paper comes in pretty pastel shades. There is good medical sense in wiping one's rear-end after defecation, for that way germs that might otherwise be lingering on your body are taken away. But there is absolutely no medical reason why the toilet paper has to be in a nice shade of pink or blue. The reasons why we like such coloured papers are *purely* 'cultural' in nature, and derive from the context created by modern toiletry culture. In a world where we have learned to feel very uneasy and queasy about our bodies' capacities to produce faeces, we make this unpleasant fact more bearable by generally referring in indirect and euphemistic ways to toiletry matters. Instead of referring to the place of defecation as a 'shittery' (thus revealing what its real purpose is), we call it a 'water closet', or a 'lavatory', or even more coyly, 'the little girl's (or boy's) room'. In a cultural situation characterized by the norms of a strict toiletry culture, to refer more directly to faecal matters would remind us too much of what we are trying to forget about ourselves and to keep hidden from the view of others. Just like the phrase 'water closet', coloured toilet paper is a euphemism, a way of dealing in more manageable and pleasant ways with something we find deeply unpleasant because cultural norms have defined it that way. Because the paper is coloured in what we take to be nice shades, it helps to make an unmentionable act that little bit more tolerable and pleasant. As a result, something as everyday as toilet paper clearly reveals the marks of wider cultural forces that are at work in modern societies.

THE CULTURED BODY

As we have seen, Freud held that cultural norms and values were in certain ways the *enemies* of the sexual and excretory dispositions of our bodies, in that the latter were under the whip of the former. But there is another way of thinking about the relationship between culture on the one side and our bodies on the other. In this way of thinking, cultural forces do not just *control* the human body, they also *shape* it. The cultural contexts in which a person is both brought up in childhood, and operates within in adulthood, profoundly shape how that person makes use of their body – that is, how they walk, talk, run, throw, lift and do all the things that enable them to live from day to day. These things are not wholly biologically determined, but are shaped and influenced by the cultural milieu within which a person lives.

This is a view of everyday life put forward by the early twentieth-century French sociologist Marcel Mauss. For Mauss (1979: 102) there is no completely 'natural' way for a person to use their body. For example, 'the positions of the arms and hands while walking form a social idiosyncrasy, they are not simply a product of some purely individual ... arrangements and mechanisms' (ibid.: 100). Thus how a person walks is not just a product of their biology. Rather, in walking, running and other 'physical' movements, the person always uses their body in ways that are *learned*. Each of us in childhood learns to imitate the ways of bodily comportment that are characteristic of the people around us. As Mauss (ibid.) puts it, the 'individual borrows the series of movements which constitute' his or her particular ways of using the body 'from the action[s] executed in front of him [or her] by other [people]'. The individual learns how to 'inhabit' and use his or her body through being influenced, partly consciously but mostly unconsciously, by the people around the individual. These people in turn have learned to use their bodies in particular ways, ways that are expressive of their group's culture. Each generation passes on to its offspring its 'body culture' – the forms of bodily movement and action that are expressive of the cultural life of the group, or as Mauss calls them, 'body techniques'. Body techniques learned from the group tend to be experienced and enacted by the individual unconsciously rather than consciously, he or she generally feeling that the specific ways bodies move are just 'natural'. But of course these ways are not just 'natural', because they have been created by the culture of the group to which the person belongs. (Here we have the specifically bodily dimension of the taken-for-granted cultural milieu that is the 'life-world', a notion that I mentioned in the Introduction to this book.)

Mauss argues that all people in a particular social group will be brought up in such a way that they will operate according to the body techniques of that group. Their ways of running, walking, jumping, eating, blowing their noses, burping, and so on, and also what they think about those activities (e.g. whether burping is felt to be rude or not), will be expressive of the cultural norms of the group by which they were reared. As different societies have different cultural norms, body techniques that are acceptable in one society might be unacceptable in another. For example, in one society belching at the end of a meal could be taken as a sign of having enjoyed the food, but in another society could be understood as a very rude and uncouth act.

This situation also applies *within* a particular society. What is acceptable and unacceptable in terms of body techniques varies from one social context to another. Within a complex society, there will be different sets of cultural norms as to how the body is to act, which vary according to social context. Mauss recognized that in a society made up of different types of social group, a person is enculturated into operating with the body techniques of the particular group they have been born into or are otherwise part of. Mauss (ibid.: 101) refers to the set of body techniques associated with a particular social group as being part of that group's *habitus*. What he means by this is that each social group has a distinctive *lifestyle*. This lifestyle is produced by the particular social conditions of the group (e.g. if it is an elite group or part of the 'lower orders'). The habitus is made up of particular ways of thinking, feeling and acting that are characteristic of the group. Each person in the group *embodies* those ways of thinking, feeling and acting. Another way of saying this is that the social group instils its cultural values not just into the *minds* of each of its members, but into their *bodies* too. On this view, a person's mind and body are not two separate things. They are both complementary to each other, because they have both been culturally shaped by the norms of the group. How you think and how you act physically are both expressions of the cultural norms, the habitus, of the group you are part of. This has profound ramifications for how people act and interact on an everyday basis.

GENDER AND BODY TECHNIQUES

We might say that each human body, and thus the everyday activities characteristic of it and enacted through it, is 'sculpted' by the particular cultural context a person is brought up and lives within. In this section I will examine how the culturally induced body techniques of particular social groups shape the ways in which different sorts of bodies act within particular day-to-day contexts. I will in particular examine how cultural forces can shape bodies in specifically gendered ways. In the next section I will look at how social class can be said to be implicated in the mundane ways in which bodies operate in the world around them.

Consider the following event that occurred at the beginning of the 1994 season in American baseball. Photographs of President Bill Clinton throwing the ceremonial first pitch of the season were carried in most US newspapers. At about the same time, but in another venue, Hillary Clinton was also photographed carrying out the same sporting activity. Next day, some newspapers carried the two photographs together. A striking difference was thus made apparent in the Clintons' styles of throwing. The President 'had turned his shoulders sideways to the plate in preparation for delivery [and brought] ... the ball forward from behind his head in a clean-looking throwing action' (Fallows, 1996: unpaginated). Conversely, Hillary was shown throwing the ball with her 'body facing the target, rather than rotating [her] shoulders and hips ninety degrees away from the target and then swinging them around in order to accelerate the ball' (ibid.). Consequently, even to the gaze of an uneducated baseball observer, the President seemed to be throwing quite effectively, while the First Lady looked very ineffective indeed in the way she was standing and moving. It seemed clear that she was, as the saying goes, 'throwing like a girl'. Was this just a result of 'natural' ineptitude on Hillary's part?

According to the view we will now consider, Hillary was not in fact 'naturally' a worse thrower than her husband. Her less than impressive performance was due not to *individual* incompetence, but to the culturally induced body techniques that modern Western societies inculcate into all women. Hillary was playing baseball badly not because of any 'essential' physical failings on her part, but because she had been raised in a cultural milieu that socializes women to move in certain ways, while it teaches men to move in other ways.

A striking feature of watching children play sports is observing how often girls and boys play the same games rather differently. Girls tend to throw things and run about in ways we regard as more 'feminine', whereas boys tend to do the same things in what we think of as more 'masculine' ways. The key issue here might be that while males tend to use their *whole* bodies when doing something like throwing a ball, girls tend only to use the body parts most directly relevant to the activity, such as the arm in the case of throwing. Therefore boys often seem to be 'better' throwers as they seem able to concentrate the energies of their total bodies in the act, whereas girls seem to perform comparatively worse because they seem to lack this capacity. The motion of the boys in something like throwing tends to seem more fluid than that of girls, which tends to be more jerky and irregular.

Such differences in posture and motility are perhaps not the result of 'natural' differences in body shape or size between males and females, but instead are due to processes of socialization, where boys learn different bodily skills and capacities for movement than do girls. This learning process can shape profoundly the ways people of each gender can experience their bodies in childhood and adulthood. One of the central claims of feminist thought is that biological 'sex' is a separate thing from 'gender', which is a matter of cultural convention. Notions as to which traits 'masculinity' and 'femininity' involve vary from one society to another. What is thought of as 'feminine' behaviour in one context might be seen as more 'masculine' behaviour in another. The fact that a person possesses a certain type of genitals is not enough fully to determine what their behaviour will be like. Instead, people conform to the cultural norms as to 'male behaviour' and 'female behaviour' set by the social context in which they live. From being born onwards, they are socialized into accepting unconsciously, and acting upon the basis of, such norms. A central element of growing up involves learning how to be 'male' or how to be 'female' (De Beauvoir, 1972 [1949]). Generally these learning processes happen at an unconscious or semi-conscious psychological level, and the person comes to think that the culturally derived – and therefore mutable – gender norms that have shaped them are actually 'natural' and unchangeable. They are in fact not, as they are the products of particular societies at particular historical periods. In sum, ways of thinking and acting that we tend to think are 'naturally' either 'feminine' or 'masculine' are in fact the products of the inculcation of specific cultural expectations.

As a result, we might think that cultural norms of gender would influence a person as they grew up not just in terms of their ways of thinking, but also in terms of their *corporeality*, that is the ways in which they move and experience their bodies. In most, although not all, societies, men tend to occupy more positions of power than women. In 'patriarchal' forms of social organization, men as a group both have more power *than* women and also have power *over* women (Walby, 1990). In a society like that, cultural forces tend simultaneously to reflect and to justify this situation. Men are seen as being somehow 'naturally' superior to women. This superiority is taken as if it were an unchanging fact of life. In such a context, men are seen as being more powerful, strong, competent, rational, and so on, than are women. Gender norms characteristic of a patriarchal society create an essence of 'femininity' that is not a natural essence, but a cultural fabrication. 'Femininity' generally is defined in negative ways, stressing the inferiority of the female psychologically and physically.

A particularly good way to think about the influence of patriarchal gender norms on bodily activity in fact involves the examination of how differently gendered persons play sport. According to the influential position of the American feminist thinker Iris Marion Young (1990: 144), in modern Western patriarchy, women are reared in ways which deny them the 'subjectivity, autonomy and creativity' that the society accords to men. Males are both defined and trained to be physically 'competent', while females are instructed in bodily movement that is regarded and constructed as inferior to 'masculine' styles of movement.

Thus, in the case of sports in a society like ours, the female body is one that tends to be less sportively 'confident' than its male counterpart. Through socialization the female has been discouraged from reaching out in a confident manner towards the space around her. Women thus tend to be more bodily *reactive* than active compared to men, as the space that they experience through the means of their bodies feels more restrictive to them than the space around the body feels to their male counterparts. This is not a 'natural' condition, but is the result of the inculcation in childhood of patriarchal gender norms to do with the body.

Patriarchal cultural norms generally instruct women how to move in 'ladylike' ways, not just in sportive contexts, but in all the various different spheres of everyday life. Young (1990: 145) describes how these norms can influence the ways women walk and do other everyday bodily movements, in this way:

> Women are generally not as open with their bodies as are men in their gait and stride. Typically the masculine stride is longer proportionally to a man's body than is the feminine stride to a woman's. The man typically swings his arms in a more open and loose fashion than does a woman and typically has more up and down rhythm in his step. Though we [women] wear pants more than we used to and consequently do not have to restrict our sitting postures because of dress, women still tend to sit with their legs relatively close together and their arms across their bodies. When simply standing or leaning, men tend to keep their feet farther apart than do women, and we also tend more to keep our hands and arms touching or shielding our bodies.

A woman who did not walk, sit or stand in ways that were deemed culturally 'normal' would be thought of as too 'masculine', earning a range of nicknames from 'tomboy' to 'lesbian'. Likewise, a male whose bodily movements did not fit with the norms of male bodily comportment would soon face criticism as to the nature of his 'masculinity'. People who do not operate in ways congruent with norms of bodily behaviour generally experience the disapproval of others who think that a departure from these norms is 'unnatural'. While cultural values as to bodily movement can be in many ways enabling for all of us, in that they teach us how to move in socially acceptable ways, they can also be very restricting, in that we *must* conform to them or risk much social opprobrium. More 'masculine' women and more 'feminine' men can testify to the fact that, like all cultural norms, the norms of gendered bodily movement can be oppressive and tyrannical.

One might object to Young's views that she overemphasizes the degree to which *all* women in *all* social groups in modern Western societies are drilled into the body techniques of patriarchy. However, Young is quite clear that she is presenting an ideal–typical model of how gender norms can affect bodily comportment. She therefore would be quite aware of cases where, for example, certain women deliberately challenged those norms by acting in certain 'unladylike' fashions. But the point is that a challenge presented to norms is generally a very good indication that they are indeed present, and the more provocative the challenge, the more all-pervasive those norms are likely to be.

SOCIAL CLASS AND BODY TECHNIQUES

Let us now examine how certain body techniques might be associated with particular social classes. Here we will look at the ideas of the French sociologist Pierre Bourdieu (1992), who took up Mauss's idea of habitus, but investigated how a particular habitus and set of corresponding body techniques shape the 'life-world' of people in particular class groupings. In what follows I will present Bourdieu's views on these matters.

In modern Western societies, according to Bourdieu's analysis, the most basic of these class-based groups are (1) the working class (associated with job categories such as skilled and unskilled manual workers), (2) the lower middle class (associated with job categories such as primary school teachers and nurses) and (3) the upper middle class (associated with job categories such as lawyers, university professors and other high-status professionals) (further exposition and critique of Bourdieu's analyses can be found in Inglis and Hughson, 2003).

For Bourdieu, each of these classes 'possesses' its own habitus and thus also its own distinctive set of body techniques. Thus there exist distinctively 'working-class' ways of eating, drinking, walking, talking and suchlike, just as there are distinctively 'lower middle-class' and 'upper middle-class' ways of doing these sorts of things too. People in each group generally experience these ways of acting as 'natural' rather than resulting from their having been brought up in a particular class-based culture milieu.

The special characteristics of the habitus of each class derive from the social conditions of each class. The upper middle-class enjoys relatively high levels of both *economic capital* (financial resources) and *cultural capital* (knowledge about highly respected forms of culture, such as visual arts, classical music, opera, and so on, of which more discussion will follow in Chapter 3). The habitus of this class is defined by what Bourdieu refers to as *a life of ease*. As individuals in this class are relatively highly wealthy, in both 'cultural' and economic terms, life for them involves 'the suspension and removal of economic necessity' and so operates with a sense of 'distance from practical urgencies' (Bourdieu, 1992: 54). Persons in this class tend to feel very *at ease* with themselves and their surroundings, and they tend to have an apparently unshakeable confidence in themselves in most everyday situations they can find themselves in, because at the root of their habitus is the tacit notion that no one is superior to them, either financially or culturally.

This situation is reflected in the body techniques of this habitus, in that it is based around ideals of 'ease' and 'elegance', these ideals being expressed in the characteristic bodily mannerisms of people in this class. For example, upper middle-class women often dress in ways that are felt to be 'chic', and they move in ways that are felt to be 'elegant'. Their upbringing has incorporated into their bodies the capacity, experienced by them as being just 'natural', to hold and carry themselves in 'refined' and 'sophisticated' ways. Upper middle-class men often tend to stride along in a manner that is suggestive of utter confidence in oneself, their very posture suggesting self-assurance and 'natural' authority. But there is nothing 'natural' about this as it is the product of certain learned body techniques. These orient individuals to prefer certain sorts of sporting activities over others. Activities like fencing and polo are typical choices, not just because they offer opportunities to mix and mingle in socially select clubhouses, but also because such activities allow movement in relatively 'elegant' ways, rather than in the more crude ways that certain activities like weightlifting involve; there is an 'elective affinity' between the body techniques of this class and the forms of movement allowed in the sports the enjoy (Bourdieu, 1993: 352).

The habitus of the lower middle-class also has distinctive body techniques. For Bourdieu (1992: 318ff.), people in the lower middle-class are in a social position that makes them highly *aspirational*. Put bluntly, while they look up to and admire the upper middle-class, they look down on and despise the working class, and they want to distinguish themselves from the latter and be more like the former. But this desire is doomed, because their upper middle-class social superiors are always going to look down their noses at those in the lower middle-class, seeing them as rather common 'wannabes' rather than as people with truly refined tastes. The contradictory social position of people in the lower middle-class reveals itself in the habitus and its body techniques. People in this class hold themselves and move in ways that seem to be less 'elegant' and 'authoritative' than the corresponding bodily dispositions of the upper middle-class. Lower middle-class people often enjoy pursuits such as yoga and jogging, because these involve ascetic trainings of the body, constantly forcing it into 'shape'. They are attracted towards this kind of pursuit as their social position and lifestyle are based around aspiration to be 'better' than they currently are. For the purposes of 'improving' themselves, they desist from immediate gratifications of pleasure in favour of deferred rewards that come at a later date if they work hard enough for them. The reward will be to seem like a better person than one currently is, such as being fitter and more attractive. Lower middle-class taste for sports that punish the body is an embodied – but partially disguised – form of the habitus and its orientation towards aspiring to be better than one is.

The habitus of the working class likewise involves particular sorts of body techniques. This habitus is oriented around what Bourdieu (1992) refers to as the 'taste of the necessary'. People in this class are relatively poor, in relation to those in the other classes, in terms of both economic and cultural capital. Working-class people do not enjoy the 'life of ease' as people in the upper middle-class generally do. Collectively, working-class people are more faced with the pressing problems of existence, like finding enough money to make ends meet. As historically life has been tougher for members of this class than for members of other classes, the habitus is based around a set of tastes which prefer things that are 'unpretentious' and 'straightforward'. 'Good home cooking' rather than 'fancy' meals is one example of this taste for the functional rather than the 'pretentious'.

These characteristics of 'bluntness' and 'functionality' are expressed in certain body techniques. In working-class culture, much emphasis is put on male physical strength. Being 'macho' is a top priority, aggressively 'masculine' activities being valorized and more 'effeminate' practices being strongly sanctioned. While upper middle-class male ideals of the body are based on ideas as to suppleness and corporeal elegance, working-class male ideals of the body tend to be based around the notion of great physical strength and a certain aggressive use of it. Thus in sportive terms, activities that involve the ostentatious display of physical strength and 'masculinity' such as weightlifting or boxing are preferred over what are seen as more 'effete' pursuits (Bourdieu, 1993). Bourdieu concentrates less attention on working-class females than he does on males, but in the spirit of his analysis we could say that, while upper middle-class females stress elegance and 'chicness', working-class female ideas of beauty hinge more on the display of certain physical attributes – dyeing the hair with striking colours, displaying a great deal of flesh, wearing ostentatious jewellery, and so on. The bourgeois female tends to dress in 'understated' ways, emphasizing 'cool elegance', and chooses clothes which very discreetly display certain parts of the bare body. By contrast, working-class female norms of beauty tend to be more based around strongly stated displays of certain features of the body, such as the legs or breasts. Clothing that is 'loud' and often 'provocative' is favoured over the apparently more 'subtle' charms of upper middle-class couture.

CONCLUSION: BEYOND NATURE?

One could certainly criticize Bourdieu's views on the nature of class-based body techniques as tending towards caricaturing individuals, and representing them too strongly as mere products of a given class culture (e.g. Frow, 1987). Such ideas of being socialized within a homogeneous class-based habitus have also been criticized as being out of date, an issue we will return to in part in Chapter 3. But Bourdieu's ideas do allow us to see in a vivid fashion the central theme of this chapter: that is, the ways in which people use, display and understand their bodies in everyday contexts are far from being reducible to biologically determined behaviours. As we have seen, whether we regard 'culture' and 'nature' as at war with each other in the minds and bodies of individuals, or whether we see the former as profoundly shaping the latter, it is clear that apparently 'natural' phenomena, such as how we manage our sex lives, how we go to the toilet and how we 'inhabit' our bodies, are thoroughly bound up with cultural forces. What we may think of as the 'natural' underpinnings of everyday activities may in fact be the results of cultural phenomena. Above all it would seem that social hierarchies are culturally inscribed into our bodies, and it is in part through the mundane activities of our bodies that matters of social power can so deeply affect how we live each and every day.

2

MODERN CULTURE AND EVERYDAY LIFE

INTRODUCTION

It is often difficult for anyone who lives within a particular culture to
realize how odd that culture, and the effects it has on individuals' mind-
sets and actions, can seem to those not brought up within that culture.
Each person exists to a greater or lesser degree like a fish in their own
cultural water, generally taking for granted and regarding as simply
'natural' the cultural forces which are constantly present in their everyday thoughts and actions. For modern Westerners, how we think and
how we conduct our everyday lives just seem entirely normal to us. It is
difficult to spot the ways in which how we live could be seen as peculiar. But if we compare our own cultural dispositions with those of
people who live in other parts of the world, or who have lived in the
West at previous points in history, we can begin to see how idiosyncratic and strange our habitual ways of thinking and acting are.

In this chapter, I will look at how some of the ways in which we
operate on a daily basis are profoundly shaped by cultural forces that are
particularly characteristic of the modern West. By considering such
everyday issues as dealing with bureaucracies, making music, going to
the supermarket, playing sport, driving a car, walking through the city,
choosing clothes, decorating your home, going on holiday and saying 'I
love you' to someone, I will show that all of these and many other
daily activities are expressive of and influenced by the specific cultural

characteristics of 'modernity'. I will look first of all at the cultural features of a highly rationalized society, before then going on to look at
how modern Western culture can be seen as involving a sense of chaos
and confusion. Towards the end of the chapter I will consider the
changes wrought on everyday functioning by the development of what
some call 'post-modern' and others call 'late modern' society.
Throughout the chapter I will be concerned to show that once we start
to look at the connections between modern culture and our everyday
lives, the peculiarity of activities and attitudes we take to be totally
'normal' starts to come into focus.

THE RATIONALIZATION OF EVERYDAY LIFE

Reflecting upon the strangeness and uniqueness of modern Western
culture can be seen as being at the heart of the ideas of the classical
German sociologist Max Weber (1864–1920). We will use some of his
ideas to think about how peculiar some of our most culturally ingrained
ways of doing things are. Weber emphasized that, above all, modern
Western culture was characterized by exceptionally high levels of rationality. No other society exhibited such a stress on rational procedures for
doing things. No other culture had ever been quite so based around
rational principles as our own.

There are a number of issues that Weber focuses on to show the
uniquely high levels of rationality in the West. The first concerns how
people typically think and act on the basis of operating within a rational
culture based on formalized rules. Such highly rational action and
thought involves calculation of the most efficient means of attaining
particular goals or ends. This type of rationality Weber (1978) called
Zweckrational, which contrasts with the type of rationality he dubbed
Wertrational. This latter involves working towards realizing a particular
moral or spiritual goal. For example, a medieval Catholic woman might
have devoted a great deal of time and energy acting in ways that she
thought glorified God. As a result, her actions were *Wertrational* in
nature, in that they were based around 'ultimate' values such as
religious beliefs. But the *Zweckrational* actions typical of modern life are
not concerned with such values. Instead, they are based around the
pragmatic achievement of more mundane aims. A typical mode of
Zweckrational action concerns actions and thoughts involved in the capi-

talist economy. Actions in that realm are unconcerned with moral and spiritual values. Instead, business is about finding the most efficient means of gaining a particular goal, in this case making profits, regardless of the consequences from a moral point of view. Thus when businesspeople find that profits can be increased by reducing workers' wages or making people unemployed, the effects of these strategies on the workers – poverty, destitution – are strictly speaking irrelevant, because the only relevant consideration is the rational pursuit of profit. Overall, then, for Weber, modern culture is about the instrumental pursuit of given goals, through following rationalized rules and procedures aimed at achieving those goals as efficiently as possible. Reflection on the morality or otherwise of those goals is secondary, if not in fact ignored altogether.

This situation has consequences for the ways in which power is exercised in a society such as ours. Most societies have a particular series of methods whereby the majority of the population are brought under the rule of elites. This could be through the cultivation of tradition – people do what the king tells them because that is just the way things have always been. Or elites can control others through the means of religious authority – people do what the king tells them because he has been appointed by God and thus possesses ultimate authority. In the modern West, however, control through the means of tradition and religion go into decline, and are replaced by a different sort of authority. This is what Weber (1978) refers to as *legal–rational* authority. That is to say, people's actions and thoughts are circumscribed and regulated not by the arbitrary uses and abuses of power by despots and tyrants, but through the systematic application of rules and procedures. The archetypical form that such domination takes is *bureaucracy*. This word literally means 'control through the use of regulations', and it is this type of control that Weber believes is characteristic of modernity. As such, modern culture is above all else a rational and bureaucratic one.

The idea here is that people in the modern West do not do what they are told because of the *personal* characteristics of the people in charge. Rather they do so because they bow down before the authority of the rules and regulations themselves, and the bureaucracy which enforces them. When the tax inspector tells me I have to pay a certain amount of money, I do so because I realize that I have to follow the rules about tax payment – I don't obey the inspector because of some remarkable personal qualities he or she possesses. In a bureaucratic culture, it is the very bureaucratic role – here tax inspector – that commands authority, not the person who occupies that role themselves. This is a major difference from many other cultures that have existed around the world, where commands are obeyed because of the perceived *personal* authority of the individual giving the commands. When we begin to reflect on this issue, we can see a whole host of everyday situations where we do what we are bidden (or at least, where we are *expected* to do what we are told), not because of the personal qualities of the person requiring us to act in a certain way, but because of the bureaucratic role that person occupies and the set of rules and procedures that are enforced by that role. Schoolchildren obey (or are expected to obey) the schoolteacher, not just because he or she has a certain sort of personal character, but because he or she occupies the role of schoolteacher. Strictly speaking, the children obey the bureaucratic role that we call 'schoolteacher' itself, rather than the person who happens to be in that role.

The upshot of this is that we are constantly finding ourselves in situations whereby we may think we are responding to and engaging with individuals, but we are actually dealing with bureaucratic roles and the sets of rules they enforce. This illustrates the high degree to which bureaucratic principles impinge upon our everyday functioning. It is not only that there are a vast number of rules and regulations governing everyday activities – from where one should put one's litter to how fast one can drive – but also that when we deal with the people whose role it is to enforce them, they are required to be the embodiments of those rules. Each time one has to deal with an official of any variety, one is literally engaging with someone who is expected to be a walking and talking incarnation of the bureaucracy they work for. Anyone who works for an organization that requires certain sorts of behaviour from the people it deals with is in essence a set of embodied rules. It is little wonder then that Weber thought that the principles of bureaucracy had colonized huge tracts of everyday life.

Of course, in our everyday affairs, we do not just simply acquiesce to what 'bureaucrats' tell us to do – we shout at the traffic warden who seems to be enforcing the rules too rigidly, we get annoyed with the 'jobsworth' who seems only to care about the rules rather than the people affected by them. It is at those points in time that we tend to think that it is the person in the bureaucratic role, rather than the role itself, that is the issue and the problem. Yet it is also the case that our highly bureaucratized culture creates a number of peculiar problems for all those whose professional role involves them in following certain prescribed rules and procedures.

A large part of modern work culture has been created by processes of professionalization, another issue Weber dealt with. Modern Western work culture is unique in the degree to which it stresses that only certain sorts of people are competent to do certain sorts of activities. Only someone who is a 'professional', an 'expert', is regarded as being able to do the job properly (Macdonald, 1995). Only someone called a 'doctor' is defined as being capable of medically examining patients; only someone called a 'lawyer' is defined as being able to deal with legal matters; and so on. Modernity is in part characterized by a situation whereby different professional spheres of competence – medicine, law, education, engineering, etc. – have emerged. Each of those spheres is bureaucratically organized and policed, in the sense that there are rules and regulations laid down as to how activities in those spheres are to be carried out. Moreover, as a person who wishes to work in a particular professional sphere is required to have the 'relevant' qualifications for the job, educational bureaucracies have arisen which define what sort of training is required for each field, which rank candidates according to their professional merits and which give them pieces of paper which 'prove' that they are indeed qualified to do what they are supposed to be doing (dealing with criminal cases, pulling teeth, teaching teachers, and so on).

So ingrained are our expectations as to the 'professional' standing of the people we trust to do certain sorts of work for us, that when such trust is broken, there is a general horrified outcry. Every so often it is revealed, for example, that someone who was only *posing* as a professional doctor, but who actually had no qualifications at all, had been allowed to treat patients. The fact that such a state of affairs can shock us so profoundly, and the fact that forging or lying about one's qualifications seems like such a heinous crime, are intimately tied up with the high level of professionalization of our work culture, a process that is particularly characteristic of the modern West.

RATIONALIZING THE EMOTIONS

Modern work culture requires individuals not only to be appropriately qualified for the roles they carry out. It also demands that they *play* those roles in certain stipulated ways. It is not enough to *be* 'professional', one also has to *seem* professional to others. The culture of professionalized medicine demands that doctors act in certain 'professional' ways, such as adopting a sober tone and a serious demeanour. Such expectations are congruent with the role of the doctor as a scientist of the human body, a dedicated and rigorous professional diagnostician and seeker of truth. However, if doctors treated patients in a totally cold and clinical matter, then that would break another sort of expectation that professional medical culture operates with, namely that doctors are also *carers*, whose function it is to be concerned about the personal well-being of their patients. Thus the role of the doctor involves different sets of expectations that are potentially contradictory – to be a dispassionate observer of diseases, and to be a caring functionary who has a genuine interest in serving the health of patients. Each doctor, and other professionals like them, must attempt to manage this situation of what Robert Merton (1976) calls 'role ambivalence', a situation characterized by a contradiction between more 'detached' and more 'personal' aspects of the professional role.

However, the 'personal' aspect here is not just a case of individual doctors being pleasant to and interested in patients. The point that Weber would highlight is that in the work culture of medicine, as in the work cultures of many other professional roles, the personal sympathy the professionals display towards those they are dealing with is itself demanded by a highly rationalized professional ethos. In other words, it is the medical bureaucracy itself which demands a certain degree – but not too much – of human empathy in the doctor's role. Empathy and the 'human touch' are themselves demanded and dictated by a bureaucratic organization of professional labour. Showing oneself as a concerned person is as regulated and bureaucratized as much as displaying one's professional credentials and adopting a sober and serious tone when dealing with patients and clients.

The general point we can draw here is that in modern work culture, it is often the case that emotional responses, the last thing we would think of as being 'bureaucratic' in nature, are themselves both required and enforced by bureaucratic regulations and rational principles. For example, airline cabin staff are rigorously trained and drilled in exhibiting friendly and upbeat emotions to customers (Hochschild, 2003). There are professionalized 'feeling rules' laid down for people in certain work situations to follow, so that their emotional responses to patients, customers, and so on follow certain prescribed, predictable patterns, prescription and predictability of actions being hallmarks of bureaucratic ways of organizing people. An important feature of modernity is the degree to which bureaucratic procedures lay down the template for how we should act in everyday situations, and how we are to manage our emotions in line with certain identified stipulations. The extent to which rationalized rules and regulations have penetrated our inner forms of functioning, even to shaping our emotional lives, is a key question that we have to ask of modern Western culture in general, and work culture in particular.

If we follow Weber's lead, then we can see all sorts of particular facets of modern life as rationalized and bureaucratized, even those which seem the most emotionally charged or expressive of free and unfettered individual expression. For example, nothing seems to characterize a person freely and creatively expressing themselves more than writing or performing a piece of music. And if people in an audience respond to the music in an emotionally charged way, then we might think that we were in the presence of an aspect of life that has not been brought under the sway of rationalized rules and procedures. Yet as Weber (1958) showed, Western music-making is incredibly subject to rationalization processes. After all, music is written down in a special language of its own. If we consider what one has to do in order to become a 'professional' musician playing classical music, one must go through training in the musical educational bureaucracy in order to learn how to read that language and how to 'speak' in it oneself (i.e. how to play and/or compose). Just like a doctor or a lawyer, at the end of one's training one gets a qualification that marks one out as a 'professional', suitably qualified to enter into the professionalized sphere of musicianship.

If one develops a career as a composer or conductor for 'classical' orchestras, then one has to become, despite the 'creative genius' image such jobs have attached to them, a sort of musical bureaucrat. This is because Western music over the last several hundred years has been *polyvocal* in character, whereas the musical culture of other societies has generally been *univocal*. In the former case, different 'voices' (either human or those of instruments) each play simultaneously, each having its own melody. The orchestra is a cultural phenomenon unique to the modern West. Its characteristics are a 'bureaucratic' dividing up of the different sorts of instruments (wind, strings, etc.) into separate sections, each with its own distinctive 'voice', and a concomitant set of procedures for organizing the different sections into harmony with each other. Thus the composer's job involves finding ways of organizing the different 'voices' so that they are related to each other harmoniously. The conductor's job is to ensure that in the performance the different sections of the orchestra-bureaucracy cooperate with each other, such that their mutual coordination leads to an overall harmonious effect. In these senses, then, composers and conductors are rather like any chief bureaucrat, in that the latter is concerned to coordinate the different specialized parts of his or her organization. If an audience applauds rapturously either the orchestral work itself or the particular performance of it, this has been achieved on the basis of a large amount of bureaucratically organized labour and effort. What moves us musically has been created and presented on thoroughly rationalized grounds.

THE MONEY MENTALITY

This example suggests that we tend to be generally unaware of how much rationalized modern culture not only impacts upon, but also actually helps channel, our apparently wholly personal, emotional responses to things and people. This was a theme taken up by a contemporary of Weber's, the sociologist Georg Simmel (1858–1918). Simmel (1990 [1907]: 445) argued that our experiences not just of the things around us but of the other people around about us too are greatly shaped by rational forces, the foremost of which is money. He attempted to show the effects of a money-based economy on how people deal with the world around them. Money has certain characteristics, and those characteristics increasingly over time come to shape the ways in which the people who use money on an everyday basis think and feel. Above all, money is *impersonal*. It is not tied to any particular group of people, and thus potentially anyone, from those with the lowest status to those with the highest prestige, can use it. Thus money is also *universalizing*: it brings more and more people, regardless of their social position, under its sway.

Money is not only impersonal in the *social* sense of increasing inter-connectedness between people in different social strata, but also imper-sonal in the *cultural* sense too. Money, argues Simmel, brings with it a particular mentality. This mentality involves rational calculation of costs and benefits (like the *Zweckrational* attitude mentioned by Weber above). A money economy is based not on sentiments, customs, morals or values, but always comes down to what we would today call the 'bot-tom line': how much money one makes or how much one loses. Because money involves counting up gains and losses, the culture it creates and extends is one based around purely rational calculations. Things – and people – become evaluated not in terms of their *qualities* (qualitative judgement), but in terms of their *quantities* (quantitative judgement).

For Simmel, this attitude comes to dominate modern societies both socially and culturally, and it is what differentiates them from pre-modern social orders, where emotions and feelings are much more part of every social relationship. Social relations become less based around qualitative matters such as ties of kinship, and become more centred around the monetary needs of the individuals involved (Simmel, 1990 [1907]: 444). For example, when I deal with the supermarket cashier, we have no personal relationship to speak of; instead, our interaction is based solely on a monetary transaction. My sole social connection with the cashier is mediated through the money I hand over. Our emotional connection, such as it is, is not just enacted through monetary means, it reflects the nature of money itself: impersonal, formal and transient. In our everyday lives, how many such 'relationships', devoid of much thoughtfulness or sentiment, do we enter into? When I pay the bus driver or when I make a deposit with the bank clerk, I am entering into a relationship that is enacted through monetary exchange and driven by the imperatives of efficiency and rationalized procedure – after all, from the service provider's point of view, I am just another customer to be dealt with and 'processed'.

Simmel of course realized that little bits of 'emotion' can enter into such relationships – the bank clerk might have a cheery 'good morning' for me or might sullenly deal with me in silence. But these are accidental and coincidental features of a situation primarily characterized by im-personality and emotional distance. Indeed, one of the striking features of the contemporary service industries is the degree to which a superficial veneer of emotional engagement is slicked upon a substratum of impersonal relationships. When the person behind the counter in as impersonal and rationalized locale as a burger bar enjoins me to 'have a nice day!' at the end of the transaction, an attempt is being made to put a friendly human face – in this case, literally – upon a relationship that is based upon the impersonal exchange of money for services and is thoroughly rationalized in nature. But even if the server manages to greet and bid me goodbye with some kind of conviction, the doubt always remains that the interaction with me is being compelled more by the rules the server must follow than by any sense of real personal interest.

It is at those times when one has the suspicion that many of one's interactions with others have little or no human warmth in them at all that one might agree with Weber's diagnosis of modernity as an 'iron cage', whereby much of the heat and passion in human relationships has been lost, smothered by high levels of rationalism at the level of thought and bureaucratic regulation at the level of action. A pessimistic assessment of the distinctiveness of modern Western culture is that it is more bloodless and devoid of spiritual and moral content – and thus devoid of meaningfulness for its inhabitants – than any other civilization that has existed. The people who live within such a cultural context are, in the words of the poet Goethe, 'specialists without spirit, sensualists without heart', a thought that might echo in your mind as you consider the superficial and impersonal tenor of many of your everyday interactions (Weber, 1930: 182).

RATIONALIZING SPACE

Our sense of the world around us is never direct and immediate, as our experiences are always shaped in one way or another by the cultural contexts in which we live. The cultural conditions of modernity shape not only our experiences of other people but also the environments in which we operate on a day-to-day basis. The spaces in which we carry out our daily lives – workplaces, schools, shopping centres, leisure stadia and other such places – all embody in certain ways aspects of modern rationalized culture. The ways in which we operate in these places are informed by both the physical designs of those places and the cultural values that those designs are based upon and express. To a large extent, the places we find ourselves in every day are themselves embodiments of a culture where rationality, impersonality and efficiency are central imperatives as to how people are to act. We will look at two examples of spaces governed by rational codes and values: sports stadia and roads.

Writing of the history of the game of soccer, the historian Henning Eichberg (1998: 153) argues that before the later nineteenth century 'ball-games had often occupied, integrated and discovered the whole space and landscape between two (or more) villages or [urban] quarters'. In other words, the spaces where soccer and other games like it were played in the past were generally rather loose and unfixed. There was no fixed pitch demarcated by lines depicting the edge of the pitch, goal-mouths, penalty areas and so on. Instead, the game took place in a very fluid space, often the area between two rival villages or urban neighbourhoods, each of which fielded a team. The game would move wherever the ball and the players happened to go; there were no rules and regulations as to where the players could and could not go.

Eichberg (ibid.) goes on to note that 'in modern soccer, however, the relevant sports space has shrunk towards a standardised ... field serving the production of "goal results" and the time orientation that modernity calls "tension" '. What Eichberg has in mind here is a process that has been going on in sports over the last century and a half. From the loose and flexible spaces where people used to engage in activities such as ball-games, a rationalization of sports occurred. This process involved a number of key aspects. First, sports were taken out of the streets and put into special locales dedicated to them. The emergence of specialized stadia dedicated to particular sports is an important feature of the modern rationalization of games. Second, these spaces were designed and laid out in ways which emphasized that players had to follow certain rules in the playing of their games. As a result, the soccer pitches we are familiar with today emerged, with their lines indicating not only where play is permissible – inside the boundary line – but what types of play are permissible on which particular parts of the pitch. Third, the spatial contours of the pitches were standardized, so that all pitches across a particular country not only were laid out the same but were approximately of the same size. Local particularities and peculiarities were erased in favour of national – and then later, international – homogenization (Lefebvre, 1993 [1974]).

Fourth, as a result of the changes made to the spaces of play, the tempo of play altered too. This is what Eichberg means by the new standardized sort of pitch favouring 'goal results' and 'tension'. Just as the spaces of pre-modern games had been looser so too had their tempo: games could be played over many hours, there might be relatively few goals, there would be relatively few moments of real 'tension'. By placing soccer and other forms of play in dedicated arenas with demarcated, rule-governed pitches, the rhythm of play was speeded up, with more goals and more moments of tension in front of the goal-mouth being made possible. This development was crucial as throughout the twentieth century sports became more and more organized on commercial bases – the point of sports became increasingly to make money for the people who organized them (Giulianotti, 1999). Thus to get large numbers of people into the stadia, the very nature of play itself changed in the direction of becoming more 'entertaining'. To a large extent, sports became highly bureaucratically organized forms of entertainment, under the pressure of making profits out of them. As sports became big business, they became more and more subject to rational principles of organization, such that every possible iota of profit could be wrung out of them. The experiences we have when we go to watch sport or view a sporting event on TV may feel wholly unconnected to the highly rational culture within which we live. Nonetheless, the very nature of the play we enjoy is generally both underpinned and driven by a bureaucratically organized search for profit (Brohm, 1989).

In just the same way as sports such as soccer illustrate the rationalization of everyday spaces, so too do the very roads that we drive on. How a society organizes the transportation of people and things can tell us a great deal not just about the material organization of that society but also about the cultural conditions within which people in that socety live (Virilio, 1986). So used are we in the present day to the persistent presence of motor vehicles in our lives that we tend to overlook just what an impact they can have on how we go about our daily business and how we experience things on an everyday basis (Urry, 2004). When motor transport was first introduced on a mass scale, in the United States in the 1920s, it was widely felt at the time that the automobile was greatly changing the fabric of society and the cultural values that operated in everyday life. For example, car ownership led to a reduction in church attendance, because the car allowed people to go on longer-range Sunday pleasure trips than previously had been possible. In the same way as expectations as to church-going were challenged by the development of private ownership of automobiles, having access to a car meant that teenagers became freer of parental scrutiny, because taking car trips meant the ability to go to places where family friends and neighbours would be unable to observe them. Expectations about obedience to parents and remaining within the purview of parental surveillance were undermined by this new means of transportation (Lynd and Lynd, 1957 [1929]).

Yet today so ubiquitous have cars become in our lives that we tend to forget just what an impact they continue to have on how we live. The French social thinker Henri Lefebvre has provided an interesting account of the impact of cars on our everyday lives. His general idea is that our everyday lives are to a large extent shaped by 'car culture', although we often fail to recognize this. For Lefebvre, the car and its corollaries, the tarmac road and motorway, have come to have a huge impact on modern urban existence, recasting city spaces in a harshly rationalized fashion. The main characteristic of modern cities is their 'slicing up' by the 'proliferation of fast roads and of places to park and garage cars', the outcome of these developments being 'a reduction of tree-lined streets, green spaces, and parks and gardens' (Lefebvre, 1993 [1974]: 359). In a society such as ours, traffic circulation comes to be 'one of the main functions of a society and, as such, involves the priority of parking spaces ... streets and roadways' over all other considerations (1971 [1968]: 100). In a way, Lefebvre (ibid.: 374) argues, 'it is almost as though automobiles and motorways occupied the entirety of space' in contemporary urban areas. As he puts it, one could say that 'the motorcar has ... conquered everyday life, on which it imposes its laws. ... Today the greater part of everyday life is accompanied by the noise of engines' (1971 [1968]: 101).

Lefebvre's view of the effects of the colonization by 'car culture' of so many aspects of urban space involves a triumph of rationally organized and planned 'geometric space' favoured by technocratic town planners and other public servants, who work hand-in-glove with car manufacturers and other interested parties in turning each urban area into one giant freeway and car park. As another French thinker, Jean Baudrillard (1994 [1986]), puts it in terms of case of the city of Los Angeles, while the 'city was here before the freeway system ... it now looks as though the metropolis has actually been built round this arterial network'. Quite simply, whereas the roads once served the city, it now looks like the city is subordinate to the roads that pour through it in all directions. The ubiquity of the rationalized, 'geometric' order of roads and other spaces designed for car traffic in cities today involves for Lefebvre (1993 [1974]: 50) a situation whereby 'space is conceived in terms of motoring needs and traffic problems' only, rather than in terms of, for instance, green places for people to walk and breathe fresh air. The demands of one set of cultural values – the imperative to allow cars to travel through the city – have come to clash with, and eventually to triumph over, another set of values, namely the desire to make the city a pleasant place to live, free of traffic noise, pollution and concrete eyesores. For Lefebvre, rational imperatives of order and efficiency have won out over other, more 'human' and 'asesthetic' values, the sort of substantive values that Weber predicted would disappear more and more from modern, urban societies.

What effects might the victory of 'geometric' car culture space have for those of us who ride in cars on a regular basis? Lefebvre's answer is that our capacities to experience the space around us have been severely constricted. Through the rationalization of space that characterizes the contemporary main road or motorway, the car driver's or passenger's experience of the environment around them is impoverished in comparison with the rich multi-dimensionality afforded to the stroller. As Lefebvre (1993 [1974]: 313) puts the point:

> the driver is concerned only with steering himself [or herself] to his destination, and in looking about sees only what he needs to for that purpose; he thus perceives only his route, which has been ... mechanized and technicized, and he sees it from one angle only – that of its functionality: speed, readability [and so on]. ... [Thus] space appears solely in its reduced forms. Volume leaves the field to surface, and any overall view surrenders to visual signals spaced out along fixed trajectories already laid down in the 'plan'.

In other words, the person who spends a significant part of their day in the car, perhaps in commuting or working as a salesperson, constantly experiences highly controlled and rationally planned spaces, their experience of the world around them being much more rationally organized than would be possible in a society that lacked cars and the roads upon which they travel. Extending some of Lefebvre's ideas, the French anthropologist Marc Augé (1995) contends that the driver cruising through any modern Western country today on the main motorways perceives the world around him or her in a very peculiar way. Although this peculiarity is not experienced today as being in any sense weird, this is only because we have grown so accustomed to such a means of perception; yet it nonetheless remains a very idiosyncratic feature of our society and its car culture. What Augé has in mind is that major roads running through a particular country tend to bypass most cities and towns for the sake of speed and efficiency. This means that the driver is deprived of experiencing those places in a first-hand way. Most places just become names on the road-map, with nothing being known of them beyond their names. However, the network of motorway road-signs involves the pointing out of historical sites and other 'places of interest'. Augé (1995: 97) argues that therefore 'motorway travel is … doubly remarkable: it avoids, for functional reasons, all the principal places to which it takes us; and it makes comments on them'. The type of perception formed by car culture involves the experiencing of great swathes of countryside and cityscape just as a series of abstract signs periodically flashing by. In similar fashion to an airline passenger, the driver is allowed by the rationalization and geometricization of space to cover vast distances without experiencing or in any deep way engaging with the specific locales he or she is passing through. Space has become flattened out and abstracted, rationalized and depersonalized. This sort of experience Augé claims is all too characteristic of modern culture, as we will see again in Chapter 4.

The final issue that we will look at concerning the rationalization of space in car culture involves the degree to which the latter contains within it *irrationalities* as well as rational control and organization. Max Weber long ago said that what seems rational from one point of view can seem very irrational from another. For example, it is from one point of view very rational to gain profits from environmentally-unfriendly industrial activities. But looked at in light of long-term human survival on this planet, it may be very irrational to engage in activities that lead to global warming, depletion of the ozone layer, and so on. For Lefebvre, clearly car use is 'rational' in that it is an efficient and fast means of transporting people and things. But there are other ways in which the rationalization of space in car culture is very irrational.

First of all, the car privatizes people's movements, placing them in their own little bubble, away from other people: 'motorized traffic enables people and objects to congregate and mix without meeting, thus constituting a striking example of simultaneity without exchange, each element enclosed in its own compartment, tucked away in its shell'. The outcome of this separation of people into their own little automotive units is that 'such conditions contribute to the disintegration of city life and foster a ... "psychosis" that is peculiar to the motorist' (Lefebvre, 1971 [1968]: 101). What Lefebvre has in mind here are phenomena such as 'road rage' and other incidences of selfish and aggressive behaviour on the roads. Car culture isolates people, diminishing a sense of communality and fellow-feeling, turning even the most gentle person into a more aggressive and selfish character, oriented towards overtaking and cutting other drivers up, but getting very annoyed when this sort of thing is done to them by others. As Bosquet (1977 [1973]: 21) puts it, 'mass motoring ... creat[es] and nourish[es] within the individual the illusion that he [or she] can prevail and advance himself *at everyone's expense.* The brutal, competitive egotism of the driver symbolically murdering the "idiots" obstructing his headlong passage through the traffic' is the extreme embodiment of the psychological effects of car culture.

Thus while car culture is rational in the sense it is oriented around rapid and efficient transportation, it also involves a privatization of everyday experience that encourages selfish, and often aggressive, behaviours. This is highly paradoxical, not least because the roads are spaces where individual drivers have to follow a whole series of rules and prescriptions, and are required to learn these and are tested upon them before being allowed to drive legally. Yet despite this high level of regulation of the driver on the roads, car culture also involves highly individualistic elements, and these can come into conflict with the rationalized rules and regulations of the Highway Code. Lefebvre (1971 [1968]: 102) argues that it is precisely because there are so many rules and regulations that constrain individuals in modern societies in general, and on the roads in particular, that drivers seek to win 'some individuality for themselves by reference to the power and handling capacities of their vehicles ... the car ... thus [is part] of regulated forms of everyday practice, [yet] nonetheless it creates its own illusions of "freedom" '.

It is precisely because modern life in general, and life on the roads more specifically, is so governed by rational rules that the car exists as a means of attempting to express one's individuality. This is not only through the means of buying a car that looks expensive or flash; it is also achieved by taking little risks here and there, such as speeding a little when it seems the police and speed cameras are not present, or parking on yellow lines, or a whole host of other small infringements of road rules. Like Weber, Lefebvre believes that modern Western culture is incredibly constraining of the individual through a plethora of rules that have to be followed. Thus minor traffic offences, plus more serious instances of 'bad driving' and phenomena such as road rage which lead to death and injury, are themselves the responses on behalf of individuals to a highly bureaucratically regulated cultural context. As he puts the point rather dramatically, 'the motor-car with its retinue of wounded and dead, its trail of blood, is all that remains of ... excitement and hazard' in everyday life (Lefebvre, 1971 [1968]: 101). While we may disagree with some of what Lefebvre is arguing, he has nonetheless allowed us to see how everyday infringements of the rules of driving may be in part generated by a culture of hyper-rationalization and privatization of experience and movement. More generally, he has allowed us to connect individuals' actions to the wider cultural context in which those individuals are constrained to operate.

CULTURE AND CHAOS

Thus far I have emphasized the regulatory and controlling nature of modern culture. However, it is important to realize that the cultural situation of modernity may be just as much about movement, change and uncertainty as it is about rationalized procedures of classification and regulation.

Karl Marx captured this point well about 150 years ago when he attempted to describe verbally the ways in which capitalist society was in the process of destroying an older, more stable and unchanging social and cultural order in favour of a cultural milieu of constant flux and upheaval. For Marx (1983 [1848]): 207), the essence of modern capitalist society was describable in this way:

> Constant revolutionizing of production, uninterrupted disturbance of all social relations, everlasting uncertainty and agitation … All fixed, fast-frozen relationships … are swept away, all new-formed ones become obsolete before they can ossify. All that is solid melts into air, all that is holy is profaned.

The point Marx was making here was that as a society, capitalist modernity did not let anything remain very stable or secure for very long. If one looked at a large city like London in the last half of the nineteenth century, the thing one would be most struck by would be the frenetic nature of life in the urban environment. Everywhere people would be engaged in all sorts of activities, from cleaning chimneys to writing up ledgers, from nursing the sick to hauling goods out of ships newly embarked at the docks, and driving trains and buses. One would also be struck by how quickly the physical landscape of the city changed – as one slum area was pulled down, another would appear in a previously 'respectable' area. New buildings would constantly be erected just as other, older structures were pulled down. All the time and at an ever-more rapid rate, roads would be extended and improved, shops would spring up selling new sorts of consumer luxuries, and new railway lines would be laid, bringing faster communications to evermore distant parts (Berman, 1983).

If the physical infrastructure of cities was in a state of constant alteration, so too was the cultural situation (Gilloch, 1997). In the department stores that were beginning to appear in the larger cities, a whole series of new fashion designs came into being, were in vogue for a while and then were replaced by new looks and styles. The same was true of the world of ideas and opinions – fads and vogues would come into being amongst different sectors of the population, only to be immediately superseded by new crazes and fashions. Partly such rapid developments and alterations in what people thought and were interested in were fostered and transmitted by newspapers and magazines, which were relatively cheap and which, because of increasing levels of literacy among the population at large, were reaching a mass audience for the first time (Thompson, 1995). Readers were increasingly exposed to a whole array of different viewpoints and opinions, on matters ranging from world politics to gardening. Modern culture, therefore, could be seen as comprised of a dizzying array of different potentials and possibilities, ever changing and uncertain, nothing seeming to last more than momentarily, before the kaleidoscope of culture changed once more. This is a far cry from the cultural situation of 'traditional' societies, where changes in ideas and attitudes occur on the whole slowly and incrementally. The unique aspect of modern culture could be said to lie in its capacities for rapid alteration and in the sense of uncertainty that state of affairs brings with it. Nothing is felt ever to be fully certain, secure or fixed.

We have already looked at the ideas that Simmel had about the impersonal nature of social relations in modern society. Simmel also made a connection between the impersonal ways people in big cities relate to each other and the huge variety of different ideas, attitudes, opinions and lifestyles that circulate in modern urban environments. For Simmel (1950), the modern city is an arena where a vast number of stimuli are constantly bombarding us. If we walk through the streets of central London or New York, we are bombarded by a vast array of sights and sounds – possibly smells too – that can capture our attention. Advertising hoardings invite us to consider the delights of a certain perfume or the latest movie. Shop-front displays ask us to gaze upon a selection of the delights to be found inside the store. A constant stream of traffic noisily wends its way through the streets, made up of every possible sort of vehicle. In the crowds of people who stream through the shopping and business districts, we can see individuals dressed in all sorts of ways, from sober-suited businesspeople to goths and other members of youth subcultures. Looking at all the people, drawn from every class and from every possible way of life, faces may stand out in the crowd – the drunk haranguing passers-by, the beggar asking for change, the child crying after a parental rebuke, the man or woman whom you find particularly attractive and who catches your eye before being lost in the crowd, never to be seen again (Frisby, 1985).

As we move through the city, our attention is potentially provoked by all sorts of stimuli, both human and non-human, both animate and inanimate. Simmel's question is: how do we deal with all these possible demands on our attention? How can we avoid potential sensory overload? Someone who had never been in a big city before generally feels at first hugely overwhelmed by the experiences afforded by life in the metropolis. There is just too much to see, too much to take in. The visual and auditory cacophony of life in the big city can threaten to overwhelm one in a maelstrom of sights, sounds, experiences and perceptions. Simmel's (1950) argument is that those living in cities have learned how to deal with the problems that city life engenders by blocking out all but the most essential aspects of the environment around them. In order to survive in the city at all, one must have developed certain coping strategies. These involve *ignoring* or at most only taking in in a rather distracted manner the sights and sounds that assail one at every turn in the city streets. We separate out different experiences, concentrating on the ones that allow us successfully to operate in the city, while ignoring to a large extent all those other experiences we have decided are inessential. As one moves through the city, one constantly monitors the environment, responding to what is important — is that drunk going to try to do something to me? — and ignoring what we take to be unimportant. Thus as I move through a crowded street, I am not crippled by the sheer variety of things happening around me, because I block them out of my mind, choosing instead only to focus on my immediate purposes: do I need to step off the pavement to get past that group of tourists? Can I make it across the road before that bus comes? How late am I for my meeting?

The culture of the city dweller for Simmel is characterized by self-focus and distraction. If one took in every possible stimuli the city can offer, one would remain totally incapacitated. Thus a certain selfishness and a certain level of coldness towards others has to be the necessary response to the conditions of urban existence. Simmel described this condition as in part involving a *blasé* attitude towards people and things. This is a 'seen it and done it all before' attitude towards life. Urban dwellers tend to have a view of themselves as very knowing, very sophisticated, very 'streetwise'. Nothing surprises me, says the city dweller, I've seen it all. Nothing shocks me anymore. Simmel's point is that without this level of detachment, if not to say cynicism, life in the big city would actually be impossible. Life would be unliveable in the metropolis unless one did not have this attitude. The chaos of the life around one would be overwhelming. A certain selfishness, a certain sort of solipsism, and in fact a certain aggressiveness, are necessary life-jackets as one is carried hither and thither in the currents of urban life; without them, one would be drowned in the ocean of sensory shocks that is the modern cityscape.

Simmel's central point is that if we do not block out the chaos of urban life, it will carry us away. The curious paradox about such a situation is that the greater the crowd one is in, the more lonely and isolated one can feel (Riesman, 1950). It is precisely the fact that one is confronted with such a vast array of other people, all strangers, that one must withdraw more and more into oneself in order to be able to cope, retreating from others like a snail into its shell. This helps explain why people in big cities can seem so unfriendly and so constantly on edge as they move about in public areas. When a tourist or someone else unfamiliar with the city in question asks someone for directions, you can sometimes see the puzzlement, hostility and fear in that person's eyes. The questioner has broken the unwritten cultural code of big city life: leave me alone and I'll leave you alone. Each city dweller monitors the environment around him or her for potential threats, homing in on possible disturbances and ignoring people and things felt to be 'safe'. Thus when someone comes up to you and speaks, it is like a shock to the system, an unexpected intrusion not just into your physical space but, as it were, into your mental space too. It is only when the intruder is seen to have certain standardized 'props' which indicate that he or she is a harmless enquirer – a tourist map, a camera hanging from the neck, the slightly dazed look of the 'outsider' – that the person being asked the question can relax a little and settle down into the role of the helpful local informant. Nonetheless, the imperative to give the information as quickly as possible and then move on, returning back into one's accustomed defensive routine, is strong, and demanded by the cultural routines of the city themselves.

REVOLT INTO STYLE

The final aspect of Simmel's views about the normal chaos of city existence we will look at here concerns his understanding of *style* (Simmel, 1997). He noted that it is understandable enough that in a situation characterized by the presence of vast amounts of people, the individual would have reasons for wishing both to be part of the crowd and to stand out from it on occasion too. Very few people want to be different from everyone else if that leads to their being viewed by others in ways that are embarrassing or humiliating. Hardly anyone, I would imagine, would deliberately want to take on the role of, for example, a drunk shouting at the passengers on a subway train. However, individuals may want to differentiate themselves from others if they thought the response they would get from others – other people in general, or specific people they might want to impress – would be a positive one. Moreover, in the anonymous conditions of the urban crowd, might you not wish to stand out from the crowd *a little*, not enough to make you look downright weird, but enough to make you look like something more than just a member of the common herd? The male commuter who wears a particularly brightly coloured tie, the female commuter who sports a noticeably sexy pair of kitten heels, the pizza delivery boy who has customized his delivery bike – all these people are demonstrating to the world that they are more than just drones in the routinized and mundane world of work, they are in fact *individuals* with specific likes and dislikes, passions and hatreds, people who in short cannot be reduced to the roles modern society expects of them.

Modern culture embodies a particular tension: just as rationalization processes have created a milieu where everyone is expected to act in predictable and socially defined ways, at the same time modernity has unleashed, as no society ever has done to quite the same extent before, the cult of the individual, the person who says 'Look at me! I am unique. There is no-one else quite like me' (Budgeon, 2003). The two forces – rationalization and individualization – exist not just in tension with each other, for it is also the case that the one feeds the other. Just as rationalization processes bring the individual under ever more forms of regulation and supervision, so too do individuals rebel against those processes, attempting to demonstrate their own uniqueness simultaneously as wider forces attempt – or seem to attempt – to harness and dampen down that uniqueness. Expressing yourself through *style* – whether it be in clothes, haircut, interior design, musical tastes, preferences in cars or movies, or whatever – is therefore a symbolically potent way in which you can express what you take to be your inviolable and 'true' inner core, in the face of both the impersonal forces of a rationalistic and bureaucratic society, and the impersonal and apathetic crowds of the city. In a way, style is always a revolt against perceived conformity, a means by which a person can say to the world around them *I am me*, I am more than just the job I do or the role I play. Style and defiance are closely connected. I may 'just' be a filing clerk during the day, but at night I'm the king of the clubbers, so to hell with the lot of you.

Simmel was acutely aware of how one's personal sense of style can be an important means by which an individual can stay psychologically afloat in a context of impersonality, for it is a manner by which one can keep at bay all those nagging doubts that one is nothing special, that one is just another worker-drone living out life for little or no purpose at all. But he made a further point about style, that is both more subtle and, as far as the comforting view of personal style as personal salvation goes, rather more unsettling. Simmel (1997: 216) also argued that what makes the adopting of personal style so appealing to modern people

> is the unburdening and concealment of the personal, which is the essence of style. Subjectivism and individuality have intensified to breaking-point, and in the stylized designs, from those of behaviour to those of home furnishing there is a mitigation and a toning down of this acute personality to a generality and its law. It is as if the ego could no longer carry itself, or at least no longer wished to show itself and thus [it] put on a more general, a more typical, in short, a stylized costume.

On this view, modern culture is in part centred around a hyper-individualism, an extreme stress on the uniqueness of each individual. The pressure on each person is to prove to themselves and to the world around them that they are in fact truly individual, not mere cogs in the wheels of society, not just mindless automata lacking in character or – a typically modern word – 'personality'. We can see these pressures at work in the romantic personal ads in newspapers and magazines. No one advertising for a romantic and/or sexual partner would dream of putting down that they were dull, boring and lacked a sense of humour. In an individualistic culture, the great thing is to be 'yourself', rather than just like everyone else. No matter how banal (i.e. how much like every-one else's) your tastes and interests actually are, your interests have to be seen to be 'interesting' and your tastes unique to you. Rather than admit you are in any possible way not very interesting or run-of-the-mill, it is better to say in your personal ad not only that you have a wide variety of interests, but also that all your friends say you are 'a bit mad', that you are 'a kind of a nutter', and that you possess a 'wacky sense of humour'. All these sorts of claims will hopefully both show that you truly are 'one in a million' and endear you to all those other people looking for love, people who are equally desperately trying to represent themselves as utterly idiosyncratic and totally unprecedented.

Given these pressures to be – and be seen to be – an exceptional person, personal style is not just a vehicle for self-expression, but actually a method of escaping those pressures. I noted above that faced with the perpetual stimuli of urban existence, the ego of the city dweller retreated into its shell like a snail. In a similar manner, style is like a cocoon we can escape into in order to escape the demands that we be as unique as possible. Style is not just about personal idiosyncrasy, but also about generality, about sharing something in common with the group of people associated with a particular sort of style. I feel less pressure to be 'myself' if all of my friends and I are goths or *Star Trek* fans, because I am expressing myself as a member of the group. I retain my individuality through the adoption of a certain style, but the style is general to a group, and group membership affords me the protection of the group. I can still be – and be seen to be – 'myself'. But the 'me' I want to display derives from being part of the group made up of all the people associated with that style. That means I get to be seen to be 'individualistic' but I do not have totally to invent my own individuality, because the group has in large part done that for me.

In a nutshell, the adoption of personal style allows me to be different enough from *most* others to be seen to be distinctive, but I am still enough like *certain specific* others to allow me both the benefits of group membership – friendships, a certain sense of 'belonging' – and the capacity not to seem *too* odd, to the point of being seen to be a friendless weirdo. Goths, for example, as a group with a certain shared style – in clothes and music – want the wider world to think they are rather strange: that is the appeal of being a goth. But individuals who want to be goths, just like everyone else, are generally keen to avoid being seen as very peculiar loners totally devoid of friends. Being part of goth culture, therefore, solves the problems attendant upon both too much and too little individuality at a stroke. Joining the group allows one to be seen as 'different' from others. But the ready-made style and set of attitudes one is buying into is a group thing, which gives one both friendships and a certain sense of security. Being a goth is like purchasing a certain sort of individuality off the peg: it allows you to cultivate a certain sense of personal uniqueness, without having either to sacrifice the pleasures of group life or to forge a personal identity totally on your own and with only your own resources.

One of the key features of modern Western societies is their complexity – they are made up of an intricate division of labour, multiple institutional spheres, and a multitude of different social groups (Durkheim, 1984 [1893]). This complexity is reflected in the amount of different cultural spheres which exist in such societies. There are therefore a whole series of different cultural niches – we can call them 'subcultures' (Hebdige, 1979) or 'lifestyles' (Bourdieu, 1992) – into which individuals can choose to fit themselves, more or less successfully (although this depends in large part on the resources available to particular individuals; see Chapter 3). Each of these subcultures or lifestyles can be seen as a solution to the problem that faces modern individuals – being seen to be sufficiently individualistic but not to an extreme degree. Lifestyles operate in the same way as do subcultures like those of the goths. They allow one to 'express oneself' so as to meet the demands of individuality imposed by modern culture. Yet they also permit one to feel part of a wider group such that one does not feel like a total social outcast. They also allow one, as Simmel said, not to have to create one's individuality totally on one's own, as they allow a person to put on a certain, already-fabricated individuality.

The case of home furnishings that Simmel gave above is a particularly good one in the present day. We can think about this issue in ways that (loosely) follow his original line of argument. The plethora of newspaper articles, magazines and television programmes devoted to 'interior decoration' today illustrates at least two things. First, the city dweller – whom we can take as the 'typical' type of person of modernity – has dealt with the anonymous, impersonal, apathetic and somewhat aggressive nature of city life by retreating into the personal and private sphere of the home. An important expression of one's individuality in the present day involves what one's domestic interior looks like, what messages it conveys to the visitor, and what it says to others about you. As people of all classes – and especially the middle classes – have retreated more and more from what is seen to be the unsavoury, sometimes dangerous, environment that is the city streets, they have come more and more to regard their homes as expressions of themselves. Thus the more 'stylish' the home, the more confident the householders can feel about themselves. If my home is seen by others to express my 'personality' and the home is itself seen to be stylishly planned and decorated, then I must be a very stylish – read confident, clever, savvy and 'unique' – person myself. On the other hand, if others think – or if I think others might think – that my taste is naff and my home a pretentiously over-designed and tackily furnished laughing-stock, then clearly that is going to have some very negative ramifications for how I see myself, for after all, my style is me and I am my style. If my style fails, I fail. I have tried to express my individuality, but my tacky house shows either that I too am essentially tacky or that my attempts at displaying my uniqueness have fallen disastrously wide of the mark.

The second thing that the strong emphasis in our culture on interior decoration and its relation to the self indicates is that individuals can buy into particular, already-existing styles and 'looks'. By watching TV or reading journalistic pieces and sales catalogues, I can decide which sort of look to buy into in my living room, bedroom or bathroom: 1920s art deco, 1960s modernism, 1970s retro, and so on and so on. I can express myself 'individually' by adopting an interior decoration style that already exists; this saves me doing the work of creating from scratch my own, utterly idiosyncratic style. Each prefabricated style, whether it be in house interiors or music or clothes, is like a crutch upon which I can rest my ego, using it as a useful way of showing I am unique, without having to go to the trouble of actually trying to forge a totally novel identity for myself (assuming such a thing was possible in the first place). A further way of exercising and displaying my uniqueness is to *combine* certain already-existing styles: while my master bedroom is done out in the style of a 1970s swinger, my lounge is done out in the manner of the late nineteenth century and is intended to look like Oscar Wilde's study – a little louche, a touch decadent, but the decadence carefully planned out by the rationalizing bureaucrat of style known as my interior designer. Even within particular rooms, I could try mixing and matching styles, juxtaposing, for example, antique dining-room chairs with a hyper-modernistic table in black and chrome. 'Daring' experimentations like these can fail spectacularly, of course, but if they 'work' – that is, if the people I allow to see the results of my domestic expression like and admire them – then there is much to be gained for my sense of self-esteem.

Having a house like no one else's is today an important route for expressing the creativity, subtlety and individuality of the self. But given that one's ideas will probably have come from TV, newspapers and magazines, then many other people will have them too. It is likely that there are a very large number of people each of whom thinks they have a totally unique dwelling and a wonderfully creative and inimitable self; it is lucky for them that they cannot see all the other homes that look like identikit copies of their own. Modern individuality necessarily relies on not knowing, or deliberately blocking out the possibility, that many others may possess exactly the same sort of idiosyncrasy as oneself and that one's uniqueness has rolled off a production line. Occasionally this situation can erupt into people's consciousness with devastating effects. The strong emotions involved when two women turn up at the same function wearing the *identical* designer dress they each thought was a one-off stem from the disappointment attendant upon the realization that taste and style are double-edged swords – they make us different from certain others, but uncomfortably like other others (Simmel, 1997). A central paradox of modern culture is that uniqueness is always the other side of the coin from sameness and that the two are condemned for ever to dance a psychologically unsettling tango.

DESPERATELY SEEKING THE AUTHENTIC

If modern culture is in part characterized by a search for unique self-expression, it is equally well oriented around another sort of search, a quest for *authenticity*. Most observers would agree that modern culture involves a questioning and relinquishing of certain 'traditional' ways of doing and seeing things, inherited from the past. As we saw Marx note above, modernity seems to dissolve and destroy traditions, constantly replacing them with ever novel phenomena.

However, it is arguable that no group of people can live within conditions of total novelty, and the concomitant psychological situation of utter uncertainty and insecurity. Thus modern culture has paid witness not just to the dissolution of old traditions but also to the creation of *new traditions*. Ways of seeing and acting have been invented, by certain interested parties, that are presented as traditional, as dating from time immemorial when in fact they are actually quite recent inventions. The 'traditional family Christmas' of carols, Christmas trees, Santa Claus, greetings cards and so on, much beloved of contemporary advertisers and retailers, is in fact an invention of the Victorian era, and thus little more than a century and a half old.

Another particularly striking example of recently invented 'traditions' is the cultural paraphernalia associated with certain sorts of nationalism. Nothing could seem more 'traditionally Scottish' than the imagery of Highland clans which involves bagpipes, clan tartans, and so on. But this vision of what is regarded as being traditionally and timelessly 'Scottish' is in fact an invention of the early nineteenth century, a 'tradition' put together by those interested in creating a mythology of 'Scottishness' that would fit comfortably into the overall cultural context of the state called the 'United Kingdom' (Hobsbawm and Ranger, 1983). What we take to have been traditions handed down from generation to generation through the mists of time have in fact been quite self-consciously assembled by certain politically motivated groups less than 200 years ago. The cultural baggage associated with other nations, such as Germany and Italy, is likewise a product of romanticizing social elites in the nineteenth century with political axes to grind. It is fair to say that it was the nineteenth century, the period when modernity as a society first really came to fruition, that was the period of the burgeoning of national myths, a time when 'authentic' cultures which apparently had for ever symbolized and expressed the strengths and virtues of the 'nation', were promulgated by elites and taken on by a mass public eager for a sense of historical stability and continuity in a context of instability, uncertainty and urban alienation.

It is not a coincidence that the era of national cultural myth-making also paid witness to the emergence of tourism as a mass phenomenon. Before the mid-nineteenth century, travel for the purposes of leisure was restricted primarily to aristocratic elites. But the advent of mass train and steamship transportation in the 1860s and after allowed people from ever more lower positions in society to enjoy the pleasures of experiencing new sights and places, whether in their own countries or abroad. The point and pleasure of tourism was, and continues to be, escaping from what one takes to be mundane, everyday existence in favour of experiencing that which one feels is 'different', 'exotic', 'novel' and 'other' to oneself (Urry, 2001: 12). What the tourist seeks above all is the exploration of novel sights and sounds, new experiences which inject into one's existence some of the interest and mystique that seems to be sorely lacking in the everyday round of work life and home life, whether one is a jaded member of the urban crowd or an anonymous participant in the suburban grind. Travel not only seems to broaden the mind but also is felt to reinvigorate the soul.

What the tourist desires, therefore, is unmediated experience of, and engagement with, the true and authentic culture of the place he or she is visiting. One wants to see what life in that particular place is *really* like, so that one come back home inspired by the fact that one has truly lived and breathed not just another way of life but another way of *being*. Whether the individual tourist does or does not feel he or she has indeed undergone such experiences on his or her trip depends to a large extent on the degree to which the tour operator and/or the local tourist industries in the place visited have succeeded in fabricating for the tourist the experience of having 'truly' experienced the 'authentic' culture of that place (MacCannell, 1974). The paradox of mass tourism was, and continues to be, the fact that if large numbers of visitors go to a place, they will greatly change it. Not only will places to stay have to be built and ways of feeding the visitors found (including finding ingredients and methods of preparation that do not wholly disgust them), but also it is the case that the economy and social relations of the place will change irrevocably too. The small fishing village that is visited because of its 'quaint charm' soon becomes under the pressure of visitor numbers no longer a locale oriented around a fishing economy, but one oriented around catering to the tourist dollar (or pound or yen). Tourists in search of 'unspoiled beauty' and 'real, local culture' therefore help to destroy what they have come in search of. As the locals move away from 'traditional' occupations into the business of catering for tourists, they come to commercialize and commodify their own culture (or what the tourists think is their culture), selling a packaged and easily consumed version of it to visitors through the means of souvenirs, constructed 'places of interest' with carefully chosen markers of 'tradition' (e.g. the castle marketed as being haunted by ghosts from many centuries before) and shows of 'traditional' dancing and suchlike (Inglis and Holmes, 2002).

The more tourists come to a particular place, the more the whole enterprise becomes ever more regulated and bureaucratized. The way that the place and its 'culture' are presented to visitors comes to depend on the activities of a whole series of people such as 'photographers, writers of travel books and guides, local councils, experts on the "heritage industry", travel agents, development officers, architects, planners' and so on (Urry, 2001: 145). In other words, whether one feels one has had a real dose of the 'true culture' one has travelled to experience, depends on how well the tourist experience in that particular place has been packaged, commercialized and brought under principles of rational organization. The strange paradox here is that if visitors have come to a place in search of an escape from what they feel is the sterile rationality and bureaucratization of their own culture, their sense of escape from these things is made possible by those things; the difference of course is that in the visited place, capitalism and bureaucracy wear the masks of irrationality, exoticism and otherness. For the tourists, the experience of authenticity in culture is made possible by the very forces and practices that seem to have made the tourists' own culture both mundane and somehow inauthentic.

Of course, the ways in which tourist industries construct a place and its 'culture' may fail to convince tourists as to the 'authenticity' of the experience made available. The place in question, with its shops selling every sort of souvenir and offering a variety of different 'traditional' culture extravaganzas, may seem just too 'commercialized' for comfort. Those who regard themselves not as mere 'tourists' but as authentic 'travellers' eschew what they take to be the mass-manufactured crassness of developed holiday locales in favour of what they take to be the 'real' Spain, the 'true' Sicily, the 'authentic' Cambodia – places where the real culture of the people has not been traduced by tourism, capitalism and the other inauthenticizing forces of Western modernity. The search for cultural authenticity constantly moves on from highly commercialized locales to places less developed and more apparently obscure. But as word gets round about the 'unspoilt' scenery and the way in which life there has been totally 'untouched' by the outside world, these places too become commercialized, and 'culture' ceases to be an unreflected-upon way of life and is rendered into highly self-conscious and stylized forms.

As time has worn on, more and more places around the world have become subjected to this process (Meethan, 2001). In the mid-nineteenth century, English visitors thought Scotland was a repository of a traditional culture that had long since been lost in England. By the 1960s, touristic interest had shifted to Spain and its 'unspoilt' coastal villages. In our own time, practically every part of the world is potentially susceptible to being remade as a location for touristic consumption. It was unthinkable until quite recently that strife-torn Vietnam could be a prime touristic locale; now it is a fashionable site for middle-class holidaymakers looking for something 'different'. Given that, it is perhaps only a matter of time before places as apparently unsafe and unsavoury for Westerners as Iraq and North Korea become subject to the apparently unstoppable 'traditionalization' processes of the tourist industry. Iraqi culture and North Korean folkways will cease to some degree to be taken-for-granted ways of doing things and seeing the world; instead they will be rendered anew in highly stylized ways for touristic experience, their newness and self-consciousness hidden under an archaic and supposedly traditional veneer.

ACCENTUATING THE MODERN

Modernity has destroyed some traditions, invented others, and those it has invented it puts on display for commercial gain or for the purposes of political expediency. The issue of the tourist desperately seeking the 'authentic' cultural experience that remains forever and tantalizingly just out of reach can be taken as a quintessential figure both emblematic of and also produced by modern culture. The tourist searches for the 'real' in a context where his or her own reality seems very mundane and dull, whilst the reality of exotic others is imagined to be terribly exciting but is often actually experienced as itself too packaged, too commercial, too inauthentic and thus not 'real' at all. If the *tourist* seems expressive of the cultural conditions of *modern* culture, the figure of the *post-tourist* has often been taken as embodying the cultural characteristics of a society some like to call 'post-modernity' (e.g. Lyotard, 1984) and others 'late modernity' (e.g. Giddens, 1990). While these two classifications could be looked at in terms of their mutual differences (see Inglis and Hughson, 2003: 160–161), I will instead treat them here as alternative descriptions of much the same sorts of conditions.

The post-tourist is someone who deals with the pre-packaged and processed nature of the tourist experience in a knowing and ironic way (Feifer, 1985). The post-tourist does not seek to be regarded by others under the more socially valorized term 'traveller'. Instead, the post-tourist revels in the knowledge that he or she is a 'tourist', with all the negative connotations that title implies. Rather than trying to disguise this fact, the post-tourist positively accentuates what he or she knows, namely that what he or she is experiencing in tourist locales is greatly prefabricated. But instead of finding that a problem, as the 'modernist' would-be 'traveller' would, the post-tourist happily acknowledges that what he or she is seeing and experiencing is phoney, a fabrication constructed for the edification of visitors, a construction that has little or nothing to do with 'real' life in the place being visited. The post-tourist is highly aware of the fact, at least as he or she sees it, that in an age of global tourism, there are no unclimbed mountains, unvisited beaches or 'authentic' cultures waiting to be discovered. The whole world, from the post-tourist's point of view, has become 'un-real', in the sense that there is no 'reality' left which is uncontaminated by commercialization and commodification (Urry, 2001). Instead of bemoaning this fact, one should embrace it, enjoying the ironies involved in being aware of the fabricated nature of the forms of authenticity being presented to one, and being amused by the possibility that the people presenting that authenticity not only know it is a fake but know that the people they are presenting it to know it is a fake as well.

What the figure of the post-tourist indicates is that whether you refer to certain cultural currents of the present day as 'late modern' or 'post-modern' in nature, they are characterized by high levels of irony, knowingness and self-consciousness. Nothing is felt to be wholly 'pure' or totally 'original'. Ever since the beginning of modernity, these elements have been present in Western culture. (They are all present and correct, for example, in Laurence Sterne's novel *Tristram Shandy*, the first part of which was written in 1759.) Arguably what has happened over the last thirty years or so is that these traits have become not only more accentuated and apparent, but also less a monopoly of privileged intellectual elites and part of the broader currents of 'popular culture'.

A general sense of irony as to the fabricated nature of presentations of 'authenticity' and 'reality' can be seen in the advertising that the broad mass of the population are exposed to on a daily basis. A striking element of present-day TV advertising, and an element not present in it very much before the 1970s, is the amount of self-consciousness involved in it. Instead of merely enjoining viewers to buy product X, without drawing attention to the ways the advert itself constructed the virtues of the product, many advertising strategies now draw attention to themselves, quite self-consciously demonstrating to the viewer that what they are watching is indeed an advert. For example, a campaign to promote absorbent kitchen paper which is currently running on British TV subverts the standard format of showing two housewives in a kitchen, one using the apparently superior product being advertised and the other using its apparently inferior rival. The subversion is achieved by having the housewives played by two burly, bearded and very 'masculine' men in drag. The feeling one gets is that the advertising executives behind the campaign must feel not only that they themselves cannot take the old 'housewives in the kitchen' strategy seriously, but also that the general public cannot take it seriously either. Both the notion that it must be stereotypical 'housewives' involved in the advertising, and the idea that viewers would be convinced as to the virtues of the product by presenting it in this format, are junked in favour of a much more ironic form of presentation. Thus the product is advertised using a parody of an old advertising format, a format that the advertisers think the public thinks is now no longer viable because it is so naive and old-fashioned. It is as if the advertising executives are winking at the audience, saying 'we know that this advertising business is all a bit of a game but we know that you know that too, so we'll advertise things in ways that recognize that you are as aware of the phoniness of all this as we are'.

The case of self-parodying adverts indicates many of the features of the highly ironic cultural situation characteristic of 'late modernity' or 'post-modernity'. The irony perhaps comes from a certain sense of cultural *exhaustion*. What I mean here is that in the nineteenth century, and for most of the twentieth century, there was a shared sense among most sectors of society that new ways of doing things were always emerging and that there were always novel things to discover, if only one made the effort to find them (Lyotard, 1984). But in the last couple of decades of the twentieth century, a certain sense of fatigue had set in, especially among people working in 'creative' sectors of the economy, such as those working in the media, advertising and the arts. There seemed increasingly to be no real novel ways of doing things that were emerging, and no truly and authentically new artistic styles or artistic genres seemed to be appearing. All that was left was the possibility of 'playing with the pieces': that is, taking old cultural forms and styles, and either reproducing them in a knowing way (pastiche), ironically laughing at them (parody), or mixing them up together in ever more eclectic and bizarre ways (bricolage) (Jameson, 1992).

Just as advertisers can no longer simply take old formats like house-wives promoting the merits of kitchen paper totally seriously and at face value, neither can many other cultural producers feel they can simply reproduce already-existing genres and styles. Instead, like the film director Quentin Tarantino, they plunder the storehouse of cultural forms, producing works which present existing genres in knowing ways (the reinvention of the 'crime thriller' format in *Reservoir Dogs* and of 1970s kung-fu films in *Kill Bill*) or which take various hitherto separate styles and juxtapose them in provocative ways (the melding of gangster, boxing and other highly stereotypical film genres in *Pulp Fiction*). Moreover, such cultural producers are engaged in the same sort of game with their audiences as the advertisers in the example above: not only do they know that the audience knows and 'gets' all the popular cultural references in their work, but also they know that the audience knows that watching the film or reading the book or viewing the artwork is a game, and a very knowing one at that.

To what degree does all this knowingness make its way into everyday life, beyond the confines of the art gallery, the cinema hall, the literary soirée and the cafés frequented by those who like to demonstrate their knowingness, even to the extent of knowingly demonstrating that they know just how tiresome such knowingness can be?

The Italian author and arch-ironist Umberto Eco (1985) argues that the culture of irony has become a central feature of our times, to the point of affecting profoundly how we feel we can express ourselves, even – or perhaps especially – on matters of the utmost intimacy. A large part of the thoroughly ironized cultural mores of today, he claims, can be summarized in the example

> of a man who loves a very cultivated woman and knows he cannot say to her, 'I love you madly' because he knows that she knows (and that she knows that he knows) that these words have already been written by [the romantic novelist] Barbara Cartland. Still, there is a solution. He can say, 'As Barbara Cartland would put it, I love you madly'.

If we are aware that what we are saying sounds terribly hackneyed and clichéd – that is, it sounds to us as if it has all been said before – that raises very large problems about 'authenticity', in this case the sincerity of our feelings and the ways in which we make others realize or think that we do indeed mean what we say.

If we felt that we could not say what we truly meant, then our every-day life would collapse into chaos, because it depends to a large extent on people believing each other and not doubting the veracity and sin-cerity of other people. The way out of the problems posed by a highly knowing culture, however, is to be knowing about that knowingness. By pointing up to my beloved that I know that what I am saying is awfully stereotypical, and that I know she knows it too, I can demon-strate, in a knowing way, that I have accounted for the fact that she may think that because what I am saying is so predictable, she might not believe me at all. My beloved then – hopefully – comes to realize that I am indeed expressing my 'true feelings', precisely because I have drawn attention to the entirely conventional and predictable way I can but express myself. By self-consciously drawing attention to the artificiality of what I have said, I have bypassed that artificiality and entered into the realm of 'true expression'. Eco's ultimate point is that in a context formed by a multitude of already-existing styles and forms of expression, the only way to demonstrate one's 'true self' and to enunciate what one 'really' wants to say is to highlight how fabricated are the ways in which one is constrained to express oneself. Only a very high level of self-consciousness can allow us to negotiate the verbal, expressive and indeed emotional traps laid by culture in post-modern or late modern times.

While there is, I think, much to commend and recognize as truthful in what Eco is saying, it is nonetheless worth considering that the prob-lems proffered by, and the solutions in turn offered by, irony and self-consciousness may not affect all social groups equally. The capacity not just to live within the parameters of a given cultural context but to be able to reflect upon it, take it as just one possible way of living among many other possible ways, and ironizing it, can only happen in a certain sort of cultural context, namely one that allows and makes possible that sort of thinking. If one had been brought up in a strict religious con-text, for example, where one had had no experience of other ways of thinking and acting – that is, other cultures – then one would hardly be able to turn one's thinking *onto*, and in some ways *against*, one's own culture. It is hard to imagine someone brought up in a culturally mono-lithic, if not to say totalitarian, situation like that which pertains in

North Korea or pertained under the Taleban regime in Afghanistan, indulging in the self-conscious referential games described above.

CONCLUSION: THE TRANSFORMATION OF EVERYDAY LIFE?

In this chapter, I have been concerned to highlight some of the ways in which we can understand everyday activities as being greatly influenced by the specific cultural forces attendant upon modern society. In so doing, we can 'denaturalize' those activities, seeing them not just as natural, preordained and unchangeable, but rather as peculiar and reflective of but one way of living life. Modern culture can be seen as a commingling of more 'rationalizing' and more 'chaotic' tendencies, and this is embodied in everyday life by the fact that it routinely features the hallmarks both of rational forms of control and of deviations from it, as we saw for example in the case of car culture.

Many people in the present day claim that everyday life is currently being hugely transformed by Western – and some other – societies departing from the conditions of modernity into those characteristic of 'post-modernity' or 'late modernity'. What has become clear to me in writing this chapter is that everyday life today embodies features that are characterizable in those terms, but that it also very much still exhibits many aspects of 'modernity', the culture of which I have argued is dualistic, caught between both more controlling and more anarchic tendencies. In some ways, then, everyday life is altered from the way it was, say, fifty or a hundred years ago, but in other ways it continues to reflect the ways of thinking and doing that have been established over the last several hundred years. Everyday life is a kaleidoscope of elements that are 'modern–rational', 'modern–anarchic', 'post-modern' and 'late modern' in nature. But none of these characterizations can capture the complexity of everyday life, for it manifests aspects of all of them.

For example, the ironies and self-conscious viewpoints of 'post-modern' or 'late modern' cultures are themselves made possible by the individualistic, enquiring and critical tendencies in modern Western culture in general. They should be seen less as repudiations of the latter and more as extensions and augmentations of it. At least since the Renaissance, certain sorts of Westerner have been well able to cock a snook at the pieties of the powerful, being unencumbered by a view which equates an ironic take on religion and other beliefs as tantamount to blasphemy. However, this is not to say that a very non-self-conscious and unironic set of dispositions characterizes only those who follow such an apparently 'non-Western' movement as the Islamic fundamentalism associated with Al Qaeda. Irony and self-consciousness may well be unevenly distributed among social classes (see Chapter 3). Moreover, many people in the West continue to take very seriously and very unironically ideas about the apparent 'destiny' of their nation; such people operate within a mindset that would be most reluctant to accept the possibility that their most cherished beliefs about their nation are in large part fabrications of the nineteenth century. Many people in the contemporary West may be arch-ironizers in certain ways, but other beliefs remain fiercely protected from the slightest trace of irony. Self-consciousness can bring with it self-criticism, and that makes it something that is as much suppressed today as it is demonstrated and celebrated. It is best, then, to see 'post-modern' or 'late modern' culture as existing in certain pockets in our society, carrying on alongside social milieux characterized by dogmatic, unreflective and passionately held thoughts and imaginings that are a million miles away from a teasing, knowing and self-aware attitude towards life.

3

'HIGH', 'POPULAR' AND 'LOW' CULTURES IN EVERYDAY LIFE

INTRODUCTION

In this chapter, I am going to present some of the ways one can under-stand the fields variously called 'high culture', 'mass culture', 'popular culture' and 'low culture' and how they might impact upon our every-day activities. What I am interested in doing here is to unpack the means by which everyday life might be influenced by both 'art' and 'popular culture' and how, conversely, everyday life impacts upon and shapes them. What I want to do is to get away from a view that sees these as wholly separate social and cultural spheres. Instead, what I will emphasize is that both such fields can only fully be understood if we look at the similarities between them in terms of how they 'work'; these similarities are understood in terms of how everyday practices impinge as much upon the apparently elevated world of 'art' as on the world of 'popular culture'. Looking at the everyday aspects of both these realms highlights certain features of them that might otherwise remain hidden from view. On the other hand, understanding what 'art' and 'popular culture' are – or could be – can greatly illuminate the nature of everyday life.

My task here is complicated by the fact that whether there really is such a thing as genuinely 'high culture' that is superior to other forms of culture is a matter of great dispute. For some people, it is just unquestionably the case that 'great works of art' are intrinsically better than other cultural forms. For others, 'high culture' and 'art' are merely labels stuck on certain objects or practices by those social groups with the power both to define them in that way and to make sure the label sticks. Arguments over whether 'high culture' embodies the best of human achievements – the 'best' novels, music, paintings, and so on – or whether it is a con trick perpetrated by social elites, are a matter of much heated debate. My position here will be to emphasize how a focus on everyday activities can help us negotiate our way through this thicket of controversy.

I will first look at the claims made for seeing 'high culture' and 'art' as 'extraordinary', involving ideas, values and responses that are somehow 'above' and 'superior' to mundane concerns. I will then examine how 'popular culture' – the realm of popular films, TV programmes, magazines, and so on – can be regarded as having pernicious effects on everyday life. I will then turn to consider how viewers and readers may actually respond in everyday settings to such mass media products. Next I will look at how we can see the world of 'art' as actually thoroughly wrapped up in everyday concerns and practices, before going on to look at how cultural dispositions associated with social class membership might well be greatly implicated in what tastes in cultural goods different people have. Finally, having looked at 'high' and 'popular' cultures in light of everyday concerns, I will turn to reflect upon what 'low culture' might be and whose everyday activities it might characterize.

'HIGH CULTURE' AND THE EXTRAORDINARY

In this section, I will look at 'art' and 'high culture' from the perspective of those who claim that the latter are indeed somehow 'special', elevated above and finer than other forms of culture. For such people, there is a huge gap between 'high culture' on the one hand and 'popular culture' on the other. The gap is measurable in terms of both artistic quality and intellectual stimulation. While 'high culture' rates highly on these scores, 'popular culture' rates very low indeed. One of the most famous definitions of what 'high culture' involves was put forward by the nineteenth-century English author Matthew Arnold. For Arnold, 'high culture' was characterized by qualities of 'sweetness and light', that is great beauty and great intellectual insight. Arnold (1995 [1869]: 199) argued that 'high culture' involved:

> a pursuit of our total perfection by means of getting to know, on all the matters which most concern us, the best which has been thought and said in the world, and through this knowledge, turning a stream of fresh and free thought upon our stock notions and habits.

There were therefore two aspects to what Arnold meant by 'high culture'. In the first place, he said that such culture involved 'the best which has been thought and said in the world'. In effect, what he meant was that the term 'high culture' encompasses the 'best' works of art that have ever been produced. On this view, certain cultural products truly are genuine 'works of art'. Such works, like symphonies by Beethoven and paintings by Picasso, are just of much higher quality than other things of their type. Thus a Beethoven symphony is just naturally 'better' than a single by one of today's 'boy bands'. The symphony is more musically complex, sophisticated and refined than the pop song. The latter completely lacks these qualities, and is characterized by musical simplicity and lack of sophistication. Artworks are just intrinsically better than the cultural products that can be labelled under the heading 'popular culture'.

The second aspect of Arnold's view of 'high culture' is about the effects of works of art on the people who are exposed to them on a regular basis. For Arnold, and for later authors who have generally shared his views, engaging with great works of art is a thoroughly spiritual matter. 'High culture' is not just a collection of objects, but is a process whereby the best works of art constantly challenge us, compelling us to rethink our views and attitudes about the world. If we regularly expose ourselves to the greatest artistic achievements, our lives will be constantly cleansed by a 'stream of fresh and free thought'. Our capacities for thinking and reflecting are made superior – that is, more refined, more subtle – if we are engaged with great novels, paintings, sculptures, and so on. Arnold understands 'high culture' not simply as made up of the most important works of art the world has seen, but also as the beneficial effects these can have on our thinking and our imagining.

Great works can raise our souls to higher levels of imagination and understanding than if we had never been exposed to them. It is possible to understand the viewing of a great painting or paying careful attention to a great symphony as almost religious experiences. The viewers or listeners are mentally pulled out of their everyday existence, into a 'higher' realm of spirituality and beauty. For some authors, such as Scruton (1998), 'art' can have the same effects as a genuine religious experience: it involves a transcendence of mundane and everyday concerns, towards reflections upon the great questions of human life – questions as to the nature of beauty, morality, truth and the purpose of humankind's existence on earth. On this view 'high culture' and everyday life are antithetically opposed to each other. While the latter is filled up with petty concerns – will I be able to pay the bills that have just come in? is there enough money in my bank account to last until the end of the month? will I get lucky with that girl at work that I fancy? – 'high culture' truly is a higher and more transcendent aspect of human experience, in that it points towards the profound, and possibly unsolvable, mysteries of the universe, the great riddles that puzzle both each and every one of us and humanity as a whole.

From this perspective, the cultural situation we live in today is a disastrous one. It privileges mindless 'entertainments' over 'high culture', and the latter gets marginalized as the former expands its power and influence. When great art is not being marginalized, it is being trivialized. For example, Picasso's signature has recently become an emblem for a particular range of Renault cars. Beethoven's symphonies and other great works of music are ransacked by advertising executives for the purposes of creating soundtracks for advertising cars and soup. The most 'easy listening' aspects of classical music, the bits that have 'nice tunes', are packaged up and sold as compilations with names such as 'The Top Twenty Classics of All Time'. Each piece of music is ripped out of its original context in an overall symphony or other larger musical structure, and reduced to little easy-to-digest nuggets that have no meaning except that they sound 'nice', the musical equivalent of vanilla ice cream – pleasant and initially enjoyable – but after a while you realize they have no substance to them at all (Adorno, 1967). What were once complex, challenging musical works become nothing more than jingles and tunes to hum along to as you do the ironing. Works of art are therefore subjugated to the needs of consumer capitalism, where money, image and profit are everything, and quality, thoughtfulness and reflection count for very little.

THE ROUTINIZATION OF CULTURE

On a view like that of Arnold, great works of art are important aspects of what makes life worth living. Without them, we would be fed on a diet of cultural rubbish that would be bad for the mind and ruinous for the soul. The absence of great art from our lives impoverishes us intellectually, morally and aesthetically. Thus while 'high culture' is separate from and 'above' everyday life, it nonetheless can enrich and augment our everyday existences, if we cultivate our tastes and open ourselves up to the novel and challenging, rather than passively accepting a never-changing diet of unchallenging, prefabricated and predictable popular cultural products.

According to this sort of viewpoint, doing such things as listening to pop music or reading simplistic and unchallenging 'best-selling' books helps to diminish our faculties (Leavis, 1993 [1948]). In the words of a twentieth-century author who shared Arnold's views, the American cultural critic, Dwight Macdonald (1978 [1953]), most forms of popular culture are nothing but 'bubblegum of the mind' – they require no thought, the pleasure they give is insubstantial, and they are throwaway and disposable. As the German thinkers Theodor Adorno and Max Horkheimer (1992 [1944]: 126) put it, what transpires is 'the stunting of the mass-media consumer's powers of imagination and spontaneity'.

For Adorno and Horkheimer, 'popular culture' is vastly inferior to 'high culture' because, whereas the genuine 'work of art' generally expresses the singular vision of a single creative artist, the former is designed by committee, planned out to generate as much profit as possible, designed to reach out to the lowest common cultural denominator and turned out on a production line. On this view, 'popular culture' is 'mass culture': mass produced, thoughtless, unsophisticated and hollow. Modern society is in large part characterized by the *industrialization of culture*. With the coming to dominance in the twentieth century of mass media like film and TV, instead of people making their own entertainments, entertainment is laid on for them, mass produced and mass catered for the bulk of the population by Culture Industries. These are made up of large profit-driven conglomerates like Hollywood studios and big publishing enterprises. Every single consumer is catered for, as the Culture Industries serve up standardized products designed to meet every possible market niche: 'something is provided for all so that none may escape. ... Everybody must behave (as if spontaneously) in accordance with his [or her] previously determined and indexed level, and choose the category of mass product turned out for his type' (Adorno and Horkheimer, 1992 [1944]: 123).

What Adorno and Horkheimer are here pointing to is that so-called 'popular' culture can be seen as being based around vast and intricate processes of market research and audience testing (Stallabrass, 1996). What is served up to us by TV and other mass media has nothing novel or challenging about it. It has been made for the express purpose of being sold, not of getting us to think or reflect. It is 'entertainment' and nothing more. Once the makers of cultural products think they have hit onto a winning formula, they stick with that formula, because they know that repeating it will be lucrative. Conversely, innovation and novelty are scorned as being 'too risky' and thus are avoided. As a result, we get an endless parade of, for example, films all centred around standardized stories and characters. In the 1940s, when Adorno and Horkheimer were writing, the 'cowboy' movie was one of the great movie genres, identikit versions of it being turned out by the bucketload in the cinema and later on TV, year after year. If we look at film and TV today, current stereotypical products include action-driven police movies – where the lead character is almost always a 'maverick', out to 'avenge' his dead partner, killed off early on in the movie by drug dealers or suchlike – and 'chick flicks', so-called 'rom-coms' where after initial dislike of the leading man, the leading lady falls head over heels in love with him, and after a whole series of trials and tribulations familiar from lots of other films, they end up happily in each other's arms as the end-credits roll. All such products are totally predictable, lacking the capacity to stimulate and open people up to new experiences that Adorno and Horkheimer, like Arnold, argue that 'high culture' possesses.

From this sort of view, throughout the twentieth century and to an even greater extent today, 'culture' is manufactured, processed, packaged and sold to us, all in the name of profit. Our everyday cultural activities, such as reading newspapers, magazines and novels, watching TV and going to the movies, are all thoroughly influenced, if not to say wholly structured, by Culture Industries. These churn out endless highly stereotypical products. We may think we have a huge choice of movies when we go to the multiplex cinema or when we switch on satellite TV, but, so the argument goes, what is on offer actually involves very little genuine choice at all. How can there really be choice when everything is made to standard designs and templates, when all quiz shows are like all other quiz shows, and when every chick flick is like every other one?

Even more than that, there is a tendency for the products of the Culture Industries to be in some ways inescapable. When a new film comes out which has a very hefty advertising budget behind it to market it, one has to be living a very isolated sort of existence not to hear about it in some way. Advertisements for the film appear on commercial TV and radio, in movie review programmes, in newspaper advertising, in newspaper reviews, on hoardings in the streets, in posters at bus-stops and on buses, and in numerous other ways. If it is a film aimed at a family audience, advertising can also appear on special promotion packs of breakfast cereal and other foods, and tie-in toys can appear in toy-stores and fast-food outlets. Vast networks of advertising and distribution exist not only to alert us to the existence of the new movie but also to extol to us, in more direct and more indirect ways, the message that if we don't participate in the 'event' that is this film, we are somehow missing out on an important experience (Adorno and Horkheimer, 1992 [1944]: 156).

Adorno and Horkheimer's point was that in the contemporary world, there exist many ways in which the Culture Industries can try to make us want what they give us, even if we have in effect experienced the same sorts of things thousands of times before. Advertising above all is a way of convincing us that we want more of the same. But we are led to believe that what we are getting each time a new best-seller is launched or a new movie is released is totally novel and unprecedented. The new James Bond film is bigger and better than ever, the new Bridget Jones flick is much funnier than the last one, the new album by Kylie is sexier than all her previous ones, and so on and so on. Although we are being fed a constant diet of the same old stuff, we are led to think that every dish served up is better than the last. In that way, the Culture Industries manipulate our desires, making us desire the very things they are going to give us anyway (Horkheimer, 1972).

Our leisure time, and what we think and feel when we are engaged in leisure activities, are to a large extent influenced and moulded by the power of the Culture Industries in order to get us to spend both our time and our money in certain ways that benefit them. 'Leisure' is not just a matter of free choice on behalf of the individual; it is about the individual feeling he or she has a free choice when actually what the individual is doing is choosing from a limited repertoire set by Hollywood studios, record companies, publishing enterprises and suchlike. What you do out of working hours might seem like the freest thing in the world: you can apparently do what you want, when you want, see what you like, do what you choose. But if we look at the ubiquity of the products of the Culture Industries in our lives, then we may begin to see another image of our leisure hours emerging, one characterized by constraint and lack of individual scope for action, rather than a totally free exercise of individual tastes and desires.

INSIDE MASS CULTURE

So far, I have been presenting the views of Arnold, Adorno and Horkheimer, and others who agree as to the superior nature of 'high culture' and the correspondingly inferior nature of 'popular culture', as if we could simply take their ideas at face value. Yet we have to remember that while such views may be compelling in some ways, they are open to challenge in others. In particular, many critics have charged such authors with having, despite all their talk about reflection and cultural sophistication, rather unsophisticated biases against 'popular culture', biases they have failed to reflect upon and account for. For these critics (e.g. Shils, 1978 [1961]), authors like Adorno have failed to realize that they are making the cultural standards of the social groups in which they were born into universal standards, thus forgetting that different social groups have different understandings of what is 'good' and 'bad', in culture as in everything else. What defenders of 'high culture' forget is that they are defending what the social group they are part of − or would like to be part of − defines as 'good', 'superior', 'refined', and so on. But just because a particular social group, even a powerful one, defines something in a certain way, does not mean that we should uncritically accept that definition.

From these critics' point of view, we have to get away from looking at things in terms of a simplistic divide between 'high culture' on one side and 'popular culture' on the other. There may, for example, be ways in which we can say that there is 'good' as well as 'bad' popular culture − some of the films of Alfred Hitchcock, say, as opposed to the collected works of Michael Winner (Hall and Whannell, 1964). Conversely, what a simple opposition between 'high culture' and 'popular culture' misses is that particular works, and in fact whole genres, can change their cultural standing over time. For example, depending on the social context in which it is performed and watched, opera can either be regarded as a popular form (as it has been in Italy) or one reserved for the sole enjoyment of social elites (as historically has been the case in Britain). Similarly, jazz started out in the early twentieth century as a type of music made by poor black musicians; by the middle of the century, certain aspects of jazz had been defined – mainly by white middle-class aficionados – as 'art', with its own 'canon' of 'great works'. Even the plays of Shakespeare, apparently the most unmistakable examples of 'great art' in the field of drama, were originally played in front of all social classes and were written for diverse audiences (the dramatic and tragic poetry for the upper classes, the often bawdy comic interludes for the lower classes). It was only in the nineteenth century that Shakespeare was well and truly canonized and elevated to become one of the cultural 'saints', his reputation as a dramatist being much more mixed before then (Williams, 1980 [1961]: 193). The point here is that what counts as 'art' depends on context; what is viewed very positively at one time and place can be viewed very negatively at another.

According to critics of defenders of 'high culture', we also have to get away from the view that just because a particular cultural product could be said to be formulaic and stereotypical, we deduce from that that the people who would enjoy such a product must be unthinking, passive dupes of the Culture Industries. A very large assumption is made here that 'the observable badness of so much widely distributed popular culture is a true guide to the state of mind and feeling, the essential quality of living of its consumers' (Williams, 1989 [1958]: 12). As Richard Hoggart (1970: 32) puts the point, 'views like these ... simplify the relationship between the producers and their audiences, the producers and their material, the audiences and the material, and the interactions between different forms and levels of taste'. Writing in a similar vein, Raymond Williams draws the conclusion that 'the telly-glued "masses" do not exist; they are the bad fiction of our second-rate social analysis' (1980 [1961]: 361). The term 'the masses', when it is used to describe the vast majority of the population, all of whom are assumed to be unthinking consumers of what the Culture Industries give them, always describes *other people*, never *oneself*. We might be happy to describe other people as unreflective and uncritical, but how happy would we be to be described in that fashion ourselves? For Williams and Hoggart, as for others unhappy with a simple divide being drawn between the 'high' and the 'popular', instead of *assuming* we know what goes on when people watch movies or read novels and so on, we should endeavour to find out what actually transpires in their everyday lives, treating those lives with some respect and sympathy, although not wholly uncritically either (Harris, 1992).

Let us turn to consider other possible representations of how people engage with what can be called 'popular culture'. We have seen how it could be said that the coming of the mass media in the twentieth century *disempowered* people, in that it made them dependent for entertainment and leisure on products that had been prepared for 'mass consumption'. On the other hand, we could say that the coming of the new media allowed an expansion of people's horizons, opening up to a large number of people ideas and things they had never had exposure to before. In that sense, we could see the mass media not as debilitating but as empowering and enriching of people's experience (Shils, 1978 [1961]). The American writer John Steinbeck (2003: 391) put this point, in the context of cinema-going in the 1930s, in this way:

> For the price of a ticket, a person whose life was dull, sad, unexciting, ugly, and without hope could enter and become part of a dream life in which all people were rich and beautiful – or violent and brave – and in which, after the storied solution of a foretellably solvable problem, permanent happiness came like a purple and gold sunset. ... [The viewer] knew that he [or she] would emerge from the glory, the vice and the violence, and return to the shrieking street, the eventless town, or the humdrum job; but [the] poor ... were drawn to ... golden dreams and the promise of happiness.

Steinbeck recognizes that there is a big gap between movie dreams and mundane reality. But he also holds out the possibility that the 'average cinemagoers' would themselves realize that, rather than naively believing that what Hollywood promised would ever come true in their own lives. Moreover, he notes that the 'golden dreams' afforded by the movies can be a tremendous source of comfort to the downtrodden and the poor. They at least offer a glimmer of colour in what can felt to be a grey-hued life of general banality and drudgery by those living it. The point we may draw from what he is saying is that, despite the possibility that the fare offered up in the cinema for a 'mass audience' is pre-processed and undemanding, we should pause before we utterly scorn what we might regard as the tawdry glamour of the movies, if they do indeed provide a modicum of enjoyment and comfort for those whose lives are far from enjoyable and comfortable.

Similar themes are dealt with in Jackie Stacey's interesting study of female moviegoers in Britain in the 1940s and 1950s, *Stargazing: Hollywood and Female Spectatorship*. Stacey (1994) here reconstructs from letters and questionnaires what her sample of white working-class women felt that they experienced when they went to the cinema, at that time the dominant type of entertainment in Britain and other Western countries. In a similar vein to Steinbeck's point above, Stacey found that her respondents tended to view the cinema very much as an escape from everyday, mundane reality. What Hollywood films provided for the women was a sense that there was more to life than just everyday routines, that there could also be glamour, romance and fantasies acted out and realized. This was especially important in the rather dreary context of a post-war Britain characterized by food shortages, rationing and, in certain quarters certainly, a general feeling of malaise. Film musicals starring Fred Astaire, Judy Garland or Gene Kelly, or glossy melodramas with Cary Grant or Rock Hudson, could lift the spirits and make one temporarily forget about all of life's troubles, leaving them at the door of the movie theatre.

Furthermore, what Stacey's respondents also indicated was that the 'picture palaces' themselves were well named, the more expensively furnished ones offering a little taste of the glitzy Hollywood lifestyle right in the middle of the local high street. Once one had entered inside, and taken in the often ornate decor and the general buzz of excitement attendant upon the screening of a 'big picture', the concerns of mundane existence drifted away into the very back of one's mind, probably to remain safely ensconced there for the next few hours. As Stacey (1994: 99) phrases it, '[t]he physical space of the cinema provided a transitional space between everyday life outside the cinema and the fantasy world of the Hollywood film about to be shown'. Rather like religious ceremonials involving 'sacred' matters that happen in places (e.g. the spaces we call 'churches') that are marked off as sites which are separated from ordinary and mundane affairs, so too did the cinema act as a locale in which the everyday world was kept outside, such that the people inside felt that the experience they were having was somehow 'special' and not at all commonplace.

If money for these working-class women was tight – as it must have been in many cases – then the weekly trip to the 'flicks' already had a special aura about it, the one time of the week when one could fully immerse oneself in an alternative reality, having experiences that were different from, and in certain senses 'superior' to, one's everyday activities. Just as defenders of 'high culture' talk of the quasi-religious dimensions of experiencing great artworks, Stacey's case study also suggests that in certain contexts, the enjoyment of popular culture can involve the separation of a 'sacred' realm of unusual experiences from the more banal concerns of one's routine existence. In the age of the multiplex cinema, it might be a little difficult to imagine the shiver of excitement and the feeling of doing something 'special' that was attendant upon these women's cinema-going fifty years ago. But the feelings of excitement and anticipation people today still get from dressing up for a special event and going to an upmarket restaurant they would not normally go to, captures to some extent the sense of occasion that can go along with even that most apparently routine activity of going to watch moving and speaking images projected onto a screen.

A similar uncovering of the complexities of viewing habits is possible if we consider the case of watching TV. A 'top-down' view which regards viewing TV as simply involving people accepting the ideas and perspectives offered by the programmes they watch seems overly simplistic if we consider what actually happens in living rooms across the country (Ang, 1995). TV news and current affairs programmes, for example, despite journalists' often quite self-conscious attempts at 'neutrality' in the presentation of stories, perhaps inevitably present things from particular angles. We might then expect to find certain types of people fully agreeing with the presentation of a story (to the point of not being aware at all that it is being presented with a particular slant), some partly agreeing with it and partly disagreeing, and others fundamentally disagreeing with it. We have all probably been in a situation where someone we know is loudly and annoyedly responding to something they have just heard on the news, either because what has been reported has provoked a response in them or because they have been irritated by the way the story has been presented: 'Bloody welfare scroungers!' or 'They always demonize asylum seekers, don't they!', and so on.

David Morley's (1980) well-known study of different groups of viewers, all of whom watched the BBC current affairs programme 'Nationwide', found that it greatly depended on which social group one belonged to as to how much or how little one agreed with the presentation of particular issues on the programme. Those with conservative political views, such as bank managers, generally had no problems with the presentation of stories that were about political and economic issues (e.g. the alleged influence of trade unions on government policies), while those with more left-wing views, such as trade union officials, were very concerned with what they regarded as 'right-wing bias' in such programmes. In the same vein, those occupying more 'comfortable' positions in society, such as white middle-class viewers, felt more accepting of the programme and the way it presented things than those in socially marginalized groups, such as black further education students from inner-city areas, who generally rejected the programme and what it stood for as they saw it, namely middle-class and suburban values. As one of these students argued, the programme seemed not to reflect in any way their experiences and ways of life:

> It didn't show one-parent families, nor the average family in a council estate – all *these* people they showed seemed to have cars, their own home, property ... don't they ever think of the average family? ... And they show it ... like all the husbands and wives pitching in to cope with problems. ... They don't show conflict, fighting, things we know happen. I mean it's just not, to me it's just not a true picture – it's too harmonious, artificial.
>
> (Morley, 1981: 59)

The general point that Morley was making was that how people actually respond to what they view – or read, or listen to – depends greatly on what their social and cultural background is. How we each make sense of what we are given by the mass media is made possible by the ideas and values we already possess, both from socialization as we have grown up and from the cultural situations we are part of in everyday life. How a white working-class Tory man understands a media product could be very different from how a black middle-class socialist woman responds to the same thing. The mass media may give us a plethora of messages, ideas and perspectives every day of our lives, but what we might *take* from that media exposure depends both on who we are and who we think we are.

As Raymond Williams said, 'the telly-glued "masses" do not exist'. Rather, what does exist is a series of *negotiations* between media messages and people's responses to them. What goes on in everyday contexts of viewing and reading cannot simply be deduced from the messages themselves. Fiske (1987: 316) for example goes so far as to claim that TV viewers engage in 'semiotic guerrilla warfare', by reinterpreting televised texts to their own liking and often in a way that is oppositional to the interests of programmers and, more broadly, the capitalist system.

However, it would be naive to think that viewers, readers and listeners always think just as they please and are never influenced by what they view, read or hear. In addition to a focus on how people actively make sense of what is offered to them by the mass media, we also have to examine the ways in which certain powerful interests can indeed influence everyday contexts of interpreting and understanding. It may well be the case, for example, that tabloid newspapers can whip up 'popular feeling' (i.e. the opinions of certain social groups) on 'controversial' issues such as paedophilia and asylum seekers. Looking at how on an everyday basis people make sense of, respond to, and give their opinions of, stories they read or hear about, does not rule out our seeking to understand the ways in which feelings and beliefs *can* be swayed by the mass media and the Culture Industries. It is perhaps most sensible to see the operation of the mass media as *sometimes*, for particular reasons, having an identifiable effect on the thinking of *certain* people within *certain* social groups, and at other times having little or no discernible effect at all. Everyday reading, listening and viewing habits are neither wholly shaped nor wholly unaffected by what newspapers, radio and TV present and how they present it. The overall point here is that such habits are complicated, just as everyday life is complicated, and what they involve cannot be prejudged one way or the other (McGuigan, 1992).

'ART' AND EVERYDAY ACTIVITIES

We saw above that defenders of 'high culture' claim that a 'great work of art' is just naturally 'great', whatever way you look at it, and its natural greatness will just shine forth regardless. This ignores the fact that 'art', far from floating free in some ethereal realm 'above' everyday concerns, is always part of society and connected to what people do on an everyday basis (Williams, 1958: 127). The view of 'art' as independent of mundane life in particular does not recognize the possibility that the ways in which a work is presented to people can profoundly effect how people understand and respond to it. What we take to be 'great' in art could be as much a function of how it is presented – and represented – to us, as it is of any 'intrinsic' qualities the work itself possesses (Bourdieu and Passeron, 1990: 39).

In a recent poll of 500 art critics, Marcel Duchamp's 'Urinal' was voted as the greatest work of visual art in modern times (Reynolds, 2004). This might seem at first glance to be rather surprising, because the work is simply a urinal, made in a factory like any other such implement to be found in a male public toilet. When Duchamp first displayed 'Urinal' in a New York gallery in 1917, observers were baffled as to how such a mundane thing as a toilet could be defined as an 'artwork'. It had not even been made by Duchamp, but had come off the factory production line like thousands of other urinals before it. However, Duchamp was playing an extremely clever game. What distinguished his urinal from all other urinals was that he had signed it. Since he was recognized as an 'artist', then, he said, surely the fact that I have signed it makes it a work of art? I, the artist, say this is a work of art; therefore it must indeed be a work of art. Moreover, Duchamp had his urinal placed in a locale that was socially recognized as a place where artworks live – an art gallery. If the urinal had been allowed entrance to such an exalted place as an art gallery, and since it was sitting there amongst artworks, then it too must be an artwork. Thus Duchamp concluded, since both the artist and the art gallery define and legitimate this urinal as a work of art, so it must be one.

The point that Duchamp was making was that, in a modern society, something becomes 'art' if those with the cultural power to define it as such do indeed define it that way. But if those with the power of definition do not define it that way, then it is not 'art' at all, but something else: popular culture, mass culture or just a factory-made urinal. Those with the power of definition have a certain 'magical' capacity: they have the power to transform the mundane – like a urinal – into something regarded as interesting, stimulating, provocative, important – in other words, 'art'.

The 'magical' power of certain people, such as art critics, gallery owners and patrons of the arts, to define what counts as 'art' and what does not, is a phenomenon peculiar to modern societies in the last 200 years or so. Before that, no one had seriously entertained the view that 'art' and 'everyday life' were totally separate from each other. The terms 'art', 'artwork' and 'artist' are *historical inventions*, primarily of the nineteenth century. Before then, these terms did not exist. People in the medieval world produced certain cultural items for use in certain specific ways. Thus pictures with religious themes were not regarded as 'art' but were viewed as religious icons, their purpose being to decorate churches and to give a sense to worshippers of the presence of God (Williams, 1981: 96). The people who made such things were regarded as being just like any other craftsmen, they were not seen as 'artists'. The idea of the artist as a unique person – and one often moody and unpredictable – endowed with a special 'artistic' vision of their own, dates primarily from the early nineteenth century and did not exist much before that. Indeed, the ideas of 'art', 'artworks' and 'artists' are not just *modern* inventions but are specifically *Western* inventions too. Societies outside the West have not historically possessed these categories and the ways of seeing cultural products that they encourage (Shiner, 2001).

It is not an accident that just as religion was beginning to be less influential in Western societies, the idea of 'art' appears, partly taking its place. From the beginning of the 1800s onwards, 'art' was seen to be almost 'holy' in nature and 'above' ordinary and mundane social activities. In certain senses, 'art' came increasingly to replace God, at least among social elites, as the storehouse of aesthetic and moral values that were seen to be higher than, and under threat from, the vulgar pursuit of money, the dominant feature of capitalist society (Horkheimer, 1972). Likewise, the special person now defined as an 'artist' replaced prophets, saints and other religious figures as a character to admire and venerate, because of his (and 'artists' were generally males) privileged insights into 'spiritual' affairs and matters that were out of the ordinary. In sum, what happened in the nineteenth century was the erection of a distinct cultural sphere called the 'art world', which was defined as being both separate from and superior to everyday affairs. The latter were characterized both as lacking in spiritual character and as being dominated by 'vulgar' concerns such as making money. Arnold's conception of 'high culture' as being above mundane concerns reflects the erection of a new social sphere of 'art' that was felt to be remote from the everyday run of human affairs. The world of art and artists was regarded as unconnected to and better than 'ordinary living' (Williams, 1980 [1961]: 54).

But understanding art as disconnected from everyday life prevents us from seeing a very important feature of so-called 'high culture': that is, how the things called 'artworks' are each and every day routinely made, sold, distributed, displayed and performed. Just like what is called 'popular culture', the world of art is made up of *networks of production, distribution and consumption* (Kadushin, 1976). These networks can enable or constrain particular 'artists', depending on the particular circumstances in which they find themselves. Once we start looking at the social networks artists can find themselves within, the ideology that presents artists as wholly unique and isolated individuals, painfully struggling to bring their unprecedented artistic visions out into the world, gets seriously undermined.

For example, here is Wolfgang Amadeus Mozart complaining in a letter (dated 11 April 1781) to his father about being unable to compose what he wants, due to a mixture of social obligations to certain of his social superiors and the need to earn some cash:

> When I think I am to leave Vienna without bringing home *at least* 1000 gulden, I feel a pain in my heart. So I'm supposed to kick away One Thousand gulden because of a small-minded prince who harasses me every day for a lousy 4 hundred gulden? – because that's what I would certainly be earning if I gave a concert here. ... But what's driving me to despair is the fact that on the same evening when we had our stinky concert here, I had also been invited to the [palace of] Countess Thun – but wasn't permitted to go; and who was there? – *the emperor*! Adamberger [a tenor] and Madame Weigl were there and they each got 50 ducats! – what an opportunity!

(Mozart, 2000: 242)

The opportunity to get both a higher class audience – the emperor and his court – and more money is lost, because of prior commitments. In this way, Mozart was not unlike a self-employed person in any line of work who is forced to seek out jobs from prospective clients (Elias, 1993).

Here too is Vincent Van Gogh, seemingly the most archetypal isolated, lonely, tortured artistic genius, reporting in a letter to his brother how he – successfully for a change – haggled with a client:

> You must not imagine that I have earned anything by doing that work for Hermans; the first day I got two bills for the stretchers, canvases and a number of tubes, amounting to *more* than I had received from him to pay for them. I told him that I did not want these bills to remain unpaid, and asked him if he wanted to have them put in his name or if he would pay me something in advance. Oh no, he said, *let it wait, they need not be paid at once.* I said, Yes, *they must be paid at once.* Then he gave me 25 guilders.
>
> (Van Gogh, 2004 [1884])

What these extracts show is that artists are always, whether they like it or not, embroiled in everyday concerns and mundane social relations, just as much as their brothers and sisters who make 'popular culture' are. This theme is pursued by the American sociologist Howard Becker (1984: x), who defines the 'art world' as the 'network of people whose cooperative activity, organized via their joint knowledge of conventional means of doing things, produces the kind of art works that art world is noted for'. What he has in mind here is how, on a routine basis, different sorts of people come together to make the art world 'work'. Becker's point is that there is no such thing as the wholly isolated artist, doing entirely their own thing. Instead, such individuals rely on a whole series of other people to allow their artistic work to happen. Becker (1974: 767) puts the point in this fashion:

> Think, with respect to any work of art, of all the activities that must be carried on for that work to appear as it finally does. For a symphony orchestra to give a concert, for instance, instruments must have been invented, manufactured and maintained, a notation must have been devised and music composed using that notation, people must have learned to play the notated notes on the instruments, times and

> places for rehearsal must have been provided, ads for the concert must have been placed, publicity arranged and tickets sold.

In addition to the people defined as 'artists', then, the art world revolves around a whole series of other people, all of whom carry out specific roles in a complex division of labour. Without them there would be no 'art' at all, or at least there would not be very much of it, and it would be very difficult for it to reach any kind of public. Beyond the artists, there are people who run distribution and display systems (e.g. art dealers and gallery owners and managers), and systems of appreciation and criticism (e.g. critics writing reviews) (Albrecht, 1970: 7–8). All of these play some sort of 'gate-keeping' role in the art world, defining who are 'great', 'good' and 'mediocre' artists, whose career is on the up and whose career is on the slide, who are the 'hot new talents' and who are just tired old hacks (Strauss, 1970).

What counts as 'good' art is to a large extent dependent on the judgements made by the 'gate-keepers'. Obviously, some people have more power than others in this regard. For example, curators of large and powerful galleries have more clout than curators of small and marginal galleries, both as to what goes on display and what will receive the attention of the critics. Some critics, likewise, have more power than others to define how good or bad an exhibition or an artist is. In these mundane ways – involving such prosaic activities as to what works get hung in what spaces, and how many column inches are to be devoted to a newspaper review – are artistic reputations helped and hindered, created and destroyed. It is both institutional actors (e.g. a museum's trustees) and individual actors (e.g. particularly respected critics) who possess the power to label something not just as 'art', but as a good or bad example of its type. It is in routine and everyday ways that the urinal or the apocryphal 'pile of bricks' can get transubstantiated into being 'a work of genius' (Danto, 1974).

For Becker, whether a particular artist or a specific work retains a good reputation over time depends on whether the label put there by powerful actors continues to hold: 'a work that lasts a long time is a work that has a good reputation for a long time' (Becker, 1984: 366). There is therefore no guarantee that what we think in the present day is 'great art' will be thought so in the future. That is entirely dependent on how the art world evolves and who comes to hold the power in it.

That in turn will be the result of everyday practices of evaluation, critique and challenges to critical orthodoxy that occur in the art world every day of every month of every year.

INSIDE THE TEMPLES OF 'ART'

So far we have looked at how 'art' is made and evaluated, and how all of this is thoroughly bound up with everyday activities. Let us now see how the same is true of how art is displayed and performed in front of audiences. An excellent example of how 'art' historically became, in both institutional and imaginative terms, hived off from 'everyday life' and 'popular culture' is given by the American sociologist Paul DiMaggio (1986). He argues that 'the classification "high culture/popular culture" is comprehensible only in its dual sense as characterising both a ritual classification and the organisational systems that give that classification meaning' (DiMaggio, 1986: 209). In other words, understanding the historical creation of the separation between 'high' and 'low' culture involves looking at how such cultures were defined to be different from each other and how that difference was reinforced by keeping those cultures separate from each other, often in very literal ways, such as by containing them in separate physical locales. If we follow DiMaggio in looking at the activities of the rich upper middle-class citizens of the city of Boston throughout the nineteenth century, we see that they effected a revolution in how cultural forms got divided into 'high' and 'low' culture, by being separated into different locations of display and performance.

At the start of the century, there was not a clear distinction between 'high' and 'popular' cultural forms and activities, as both were part of a single marketplace. For example, productions of Shakespeare appeared in the same theatres as burlesque and variety shows, involving comedians, clowns and jugglers, and performances of Mozart could share the bill alongside folk music and popular ballads. However, by the end of the century, the Boston upper classes had marked off a distinctive cultural territory of 'high arts', and had taken them out of the marketplace by placing them within an organizational network of largely non-profit organizations. Museums, concert halls, galleries and other places for 'high culture' were erected, with only cultural forms defined to be real 'art' – works by Shakespeare, Mozart, and so on – being allowed in.

What were now defined as merely 'popular entertainments' were regarded as purely commercial in nature, and fit only for the lower classes. These remained in the commercial theatre sector. In effect, a whole 'world' of high culture, with its own special places of presentation, had been created, with a whole squadron of cultural police – gallery owners, critics and the like – patrolling its perimeters, saying which sorts of things were allowed in and which were not. Similar processes of separating, sifting and winnowing cultural forms and placing them in the world of 'art' or the world of 'entertainment' and 'popular culture' happened all across the Western world at this time.

DiMaggio's empirical study confirms the more general claim of the sociologist Karl Mannheim (1956: 184) that in societies where 'the political and social order basically rests upon the distinction between "higher" and "lower" human types, an analogous distinction is also made between "higher" and "lower" objects of knowledge or aesthetic enjoyment'. In other words, in a society where there are different classes which are hierarchically ordered in a pecking order – upper classes at the top, lower classes at the bottom – then there will be a 'high culture' associated with, made by and consumed by elites, and a 'low culture' associated with and consumed by – although not necessarily made by – the lower orders. In essence, the distinction between 'high' and 'low' culture is based on the distinction between classes, between dominant and dominated, rulers and ruled, people who are defined as being 'refined' and those defined as being 'crude' (Bourdieu, 1992).

The effect of all of this activity on the behalf of Boston and other social elites mentioned above was to create a 'sacred' realm of 'art' on the one side and a 'profane' realm of 'popular culture' on the other. As we saw above, there are great similarities between the modern cult of 'art' and traditional religion: both believe in 'higher' things that are somehow above or beyond the ordinary (Gimpel, 1969). The 'religious' dimension of 'art' mentioned above helps explain why there is often such a hushed and reverential tone in art galleries and concert halls devoted to classical music. The devotees of 'art' have gathered in a place dedicated to the worship of higher things. Just as medieval pilgrims would wait in a line in a state of excited awe to view the relics of a saint, so today do people queue up to get a brief glimpse of a work like the *Mona Lisa*, before getting hustled on by the crowd behind them. They have paid their respects to a great and wondrous thing, probably without being fully aware of what makes it so great and wondrous, beyond the fact of its great fame.

Galleries and suchlike places are governed by certain norms – one must move around speaking, if at all, in hushed tones, one is expected to pay close attention to works that provoke one's attention, one is generally expected to participate in a respectful fashion in the worship of the wonders on display. Even when someone slates a particular work, they are not questioning the overall expectations of the art world; they are merely saying that the work has failed to achieve the status of 'true art'. But the very category of 'art' itself remains unquestioned, even when particular works are being severely questioned. As we have seen, the very category of 'art' is a historical construct, a fabrication, but the fabricated nature of the whole business of art, artists and art appreciation rarely comes to the surface. Just as religious believers in a society that does not allow widespread disbelief never really question the basis of their beliefs, so too do the devotees of art live in a society that accepts the validity of the institution called the 'art world' and thus never really come to realize the possibility that what they are doing may be worryingly akin to sincerely complimenting the emperor as to his new clothes. From the point of view of art's devotees, only those who have no taste, no appreciation, could possibly think that the emperor's clothes were fictional and that he was actually naked. In this way, beliefs as to the validity of the institution called 'art', and the notion that 'art' and 'popular culture', and 'art' and 'everyday life', are wholly distinct and separate realms, continue to be reproduced. These are indeed separate realms today but only because our society is organized in such a way as to make them like that. In a different sort of society, we might have very different ideas about the relations between these areas; indeed, we might not see them as distinct and separable areas at all.

The argument I have just put forward is particularly associated with the French sociologist Pierre Bourdieu, whose ideas we first encountered in Chapter 1. I do not want to suggest that Bourdieu's views on the world of art are just simply 'correct' (for a critique, see Inglis and Hughson, 2003). But I think that they can help us understand the particular relationships each of us as individuals, and as members of social groups, can have with what in our society are defined as 'high' and 'popular' culture. Consider these questions. How often do you visit art galleries and similar places, such as art museums, classical music halls and opera houses? How enjoyable do you find them? How comfortable do you feel within them? If you go to galleries and similar places frequently, if you enjoy them, and if you feel at ease in that sort of environment, then you probably have high levels of what Bourdieu calls 'cultural capital'. This is knowledge of what in our society is defined as 'legitimate culture' – all the elements of high culture like Beethoven symphonies, books by the likes of Jane Austen, poems by T. S. Eliot and suchlike, paintings by Picasso and Braque, and so on and so on.

If you have low levels of cultural capital – low levels of knowledge about the sorts of things mentioned above – then the chances are not only will you probably not have a great deal of desire to go to galleries and similar places, but if you do happen to go, then you are likely not to enjoy the experience very much. You will not feel at ease, partly because while everyone else is talking confidently – albeit generally in hushed tones – about the art on display, and they seem to know what they are talking about, you may well feel ill-equipped to say anything sensible and feel it is better just to keep your mouth shut for fear of embarrassing yourself. You may feel that this is not a place for someone like yourself, it is best left to others, people you may well regard as rather snobbish and pretentious. On the other hand, if you have high levels of cultural capital, you should feel very much at ease in this world, and as the cheap champagne flows and as the canapés are passed round at the private showing, you feel no reason in the world why those around you should not share in your views as to the 'challenging' sculpture down the hallway and the 'so very jejeune' installation in the next room. Quite simply, according to Bourdieu, whether you feel at home in the world of art or wholly estranged and alienated from it depends on how much cultural capital you possess.

A wider issue springs from this: why do some people like the things we call 'art' and others have no interest in or can't stand them? Conversely, why do some people despise – or affect to despise – what is called 'popular culture' when others lap it up?

Bourdieu's answers to these questions hinge not only on how much 'cultural capital' a person possesses in their adult lives, but also upon the socialization processes from early childhood onwards which gave them the amount of cultural capital they possess. Both home-life and school-life profoundly affect how much cultural capital a person ends up with. In terms of domestic situations, someone who is socialized in a domestic situation – probably that of the upper middle-class – where the products of 'high culture' are all around – piano or ballet lessons, parents who go to the opera – will probably grow up feeling wholly comfortable with that sort of lifestyle. They will therefore like and appreciate classical symphonies, opera, poetry, and so on. But someone who was not brought up in such a way will in later life feel much more uncomfortable with such things, either wanting to be part of such a life but rather intimidated by it and the people who inhabit it (the characteristic fate of the lower middle-class person, according to Bourdieu) or turned off and at best perplexed by it, at worst finding it stupid and laughable (the probable attitude of working-class people). The less cultural capital you have, as a result of upbringing, the more you will think poetry is a waste of time and that opera is just unpleasant noise.

For Bourdieu, the same sorts of things happen in formal education (Bourdieu and Passeron, 1990). Essentially, the more of what we might conveniently term a 'middle-class education' you have, the more cultural capital you will possess in adult life and the more you will like what we today call 'art' and dislike or avoid more 'common' forms of culture. Conversely, the more of a 'working-class education' you experience, the less cultural capital you will have, the more you will detest 'art' and embrace what is defined as 'popular' culture – game shows, soap operas and the like. This is an oversimplification of Bourdieu's argument but it communicates the main gist of it.

This goes on despite modern Western schooling systems being apparently based around the notion of meritocracy: if you work hard, no matter what your social background is, you will get good examination grades and thus be able to get a 'good' job. There is a 'hidden agenda' in educational systems (Bourdieu, 1998: 52–53) but it operates, and has effects, beyond the consciousness of the people involved. Teachers genuinely think that they are being meritocratic in their assessments of their pupils. But teachers themselves have been socialized by the educational system that trained them into operating in unconscious and semi-conscious ways with 'high culture', the culture associated with high levels of cultural capital and thus the culture of the upper middle class, as the norm against which to assess their pupils (ibid.: 22). Pupils are both regarded informally and formally classified (e.g. in examinations and essays) as being 'bright' or 'gifted' because they have capacities, such as the ability to speak 'confidently' and to express themselves in 'sophisticated' ways, which are part and parcel of having high levels of cultural capital, gained from being raised in upper middle-class homes. Children raised in lower-class homes, who lack such cultural capital, are therefore assessed in much more negative ways. This has little to do with 'intrinsic' levels of intelligence. What the school system tests is not how 'naturally' intelligent – or unintelligent – you are, but how much cultural capital you have got. If you speak in a local dialect (e.g. Liverpudlian, Glaswegian) at home, this is not going to help you in your schoolwork, because school is based around speaking and writing in 'standard English', the very language that upper middle-class people all across the country use at home. This gives them an advantage: they already feel very comfortable in the school's linguistic environment, whereas children who normally speak in other ways generally feel quite alienated from 'posh' speech (Bourdieu, 1991). Overall, pupils are regarded as being intelligent or stupid, 'promising' or 'failures', less on any intrinsic merits they have but more on the basis of whether they display more upper middle-class traits or not; that is, how much cultural capital they have at their disposal (Bourdieu and Passeron, 1990: 52). In turn, children internalize the judgements made about them by teachers, with upper middle-class confidence in oneself being confirmed by school experiences, and the lack of confidence amongst working-class and lower middle-class children also being confirmed.

The upshot of all of this is that if you like what are called 'the arts', and if you feel comfortable in places like art galleries and museums, this probably has a great deal to do with your family background and the nature of your schooling. Likewise, if you do not like opera, classical music, poetry, modern visual art and all the other paraphernalia of 'high culture', that too greatly depends on what kind of family you come from and what kind of school you went to. Looking at the issues to do with 'high' and 'low' cultures in this way severely challenges the view that 'great' works of art just are naturally so great that their greatness communicates itself to anyone and everyone. If we follow Bourdieu, we can say that whether or not a particular cultural product 'speaks' to you or means nothing to you or even repels you, is to a large extent dependent on who you are, what background you come from, and how much or how little cultural capital you carry around with you.

'LOW CULTURE' AND RESISTANCE

So far, I have examined how, despite its allegedly ethereal and transcendent nature, 'high culture' is actually profoundly wrapped up in everyday activities and relationships. I have also looked at the apparent antithesis of 'art', namely 'popular culture', and considered how the cultural products of the mass media may impact on people's everyday lives. What remains to be considered, however, is the nature of another of the antitheses of 'high culture', namely what we can call 'low culture'. In this section we will look at a number of possible meanings of that term.

In the first instance, 'low culture' could refer to cultural products which fail to meet certain canons of taste and decorum, and instead exhibit qualities that are the opposite of 'great art'. Given what has been said about the relativity of what counts as 'art' and what does not, it follows that what a particular person would define as 'low culture' varies, depending on the social position occupied by that person; what is 'low' for one person could be regarded as quite legitimate, and thus not 'low' at all, by another. For someone who has a high level of cultural capital in musical terms, for example, the music of Tchaikovsky such as 'The Nutcracker' and 'Swan Lake' is part of 'low culture' because it seems to them kitsch, superficial and rather tacky. But for someone with a different set of musical tastes, based around a lower level of cultural capital, Tchaikovsky's music could seem very beautiful indeed, because it's airy and tuneful. Here again we come up against the relativity of cultural judgements as to what sorts of things should be placed in the boxes of high and low culture.

A second way of understanding 'low culture' involves seeing it as involving certain creative energies among those at the bottom of the social hierarchy – the working classes, disadvantaged minorities and other groups that might conventionally be seen as the 'victims' of capitalist society. As Hoggart (1982: 128) puts it, there may be vital cultural forces at work in the lives of the downtrodden, characterized by 'an unsuspected energy ... [and] a thrust back from the grass roots ... [involving] a kind of imaginative inventiveness that nothing in our assumptions gave us reason to expect'.

For Michel de Certeau (1997: viii), the everyday culture of the socially disadvantaged, far from being a site of total control by governmental authorities and total manipulation by the Culture Industries, in fact is characterized by 'a proliferation of inventions in limited spaces'. In other words, people can respond to difficult and unpromising circumstances by developing certain means of coping with them and certain ways of avoiding the worst aspects of what is imposed upon them by rules and authorities. As de Certeau (1984: xix) puts it, the 'weak ... continually turn to their own ends forces alien to them'. The socially disadvantaged can turn the workings of 'the System' to their own advantage, generally in *ad hoc* and fleeting ways. They are like poachers operating in woods run by and for the powerful, always finding ways of 'making do' and evading full regulation by the authorities.

An example of this sort of creativity in apparently adverse circumstances would be the person who turns the impersonal space of a rented or local authority apartment into their own home by decorating and furnishing it in a manner of their own choosing. Working within the constraints set by the landlord or the authorities as to what is permissible and what not, the renter transforms with 'their acts and memories' a space that is not theirs into one that feels as if it is (ibid.: xxi). In the same vein, workers who have ways of evading the formal rules of the factory – making cigarette breaks last longer than they should, 'taking the piss' out of the foreman behind his back, using machinery and tools on the boss's time to make things for their own personal use – have found means of operating in the gaps between the regulations. On this view, 'low culture' is made up of all the sly, cunning, unofficial and yet relatively invisible acts of those whom we might otherwise think were the most oppressed of all.

Similar ways of looking at the generally unseen and unregulated practices of everyday existence have been suggested by Paul Willis. For him, everyday life is characterized by the 'common culture' of ordinary people, the ways in which people 'humanize, decorate and invest with meanings their common life spaces and social practices' (1990: 2). For Willis, what is condescendingly referred to as 'low culture' is actually the terrain of 'grounded aesthetics', ways of thinking, perceiving and evaluating that are just as 'creative' as the activities associated with 'high culture' and the art world. On this view, ordinary people are just as inherently 'artistic' (creative, thoughtful, imaginative) as those that our society defines as 'artists'. The ways they choose clothes, select music and discuss TV programmes involves 'symbolic creativity' rather than passive acceptance of fads, fashions and opinions proffered by the

Culture Industries. 'Grounded aesthetics' are the popular and everyday equivalents of 'high culture' but they go generally unnoticed and unreflected upon in a society like ours, except when those with biases towards high culture comment upon the alleged vulgarity of the tastes of 'common people'. Willis argues that there is tremendous creative energy in everyday activities such as decorating one's home or choosing an ensemble of clothes from charity shops, forms of cultural innovation quite as vital – if not more so – than the officially sanctioned sphere of 'creativity', namely the art world.

A third way of seeing low culture is as values and activities which not only break the norms of 'high culture' but do so wilfully and provocatively. Perhaps the most famous account of this sort of situation is offered by the Russian thinker Mikhail Bakhtin. Although Bakhtin was referring to medieval society and the importance of carnival celebrations within it, his views are to an extent generalizable to all human societies. Bakhtin (1984: 96) argued that culture is separated into two mutually antagonistic realms, 'the serious and the laughing aspect[s]'.

The 'serious' world is made up of officialdom, the realm of dominant groups and classes, social elites, 'high culture', officialdom, government and bureaucracy. These seek to control, but never fully succeed in reigning in, the forces associated with subordinate groups and classes. The broad masses of the people, far from passively accepting the ideas and values of dominant groups, are highly sceptical of those claims, often mocking and laughing at what they see as the pompous attitudes and activities of their social superiors. Following this line of thought, there *is* such a thing as genuinely 'popular' culture; it is to be found in the habitual mocking of authority and sly anti-establishment humour of the lower classes and the socially disenfranchised.

We saw above that, on Bourdieu's view, the education systems of modern Western societies generally favour the middle classes and disadvantage the working classes. If working-class kids feel alienated from the formality of the school environment, where they have to speak in ways that are unnatural to them and where they have to go through the motions of doing exams and suchlike when they know they are going to end up in manual labour or on the dole anyway, it is little surprise that they can turn instead towards disrupting the official school regime. In Paul Willis's (1977) study of working-class 'lads' who were known by their teachers as the school troublemakers, what he found was a cultural situation that Bakhtin would have recognized. Life in and out of school for the male teenagers Willis talked to was centred around 'having a laff' as they put it, upsetting the authority of the teachers through all sorts of disruptive and 'rude' behaviour and generally making life difficult for anyone who sought to impose rules and regulations upon them.

Describing what sort of mischief the lads got up to in the local park, one boy replied 'they switch on the dynamo on the park-keeper's bike, "That'll slow the cunt down a bit" ' (1977: 31). It is not just adult authority figures who are mocked; the more conformist pupils in the school, who are seen as having bowed down before authority and thus are deserving of whatever they get, receive more than their fair share of ill-treatment. Here one of the lads describes a favoured practical joke among the group to be played on unsuspecting fellow pupils:

> The chief occupation when we'm all in the halls is playing with all the little clips what hold the chairs together. You take them off and you clip someone's coat to his chair and just wait until he gets up.
>
> (ibid.: 30)

It is not just the 'swots' who are at the receiving end of the lads' sense of humour. Members of the group themselves can also be subjected to a certain amount of mockery. As Willis (1977: 33) noted, plans are continually made to play jokes on individuals who are not there: 'Let's send him to Coventry when he comes', 'Let's laugh at everything he says', 'Let's pretend we can't understand and say "How do you mean" all the time.' The lads' shared sense of humour embodies a certain moral code – some people deserve ridicule more than others. In their view of things – in their 'culture' – while it is OK to tease your pals a little, it would be illegitimate to take things too far. More extreme treatment is reserved for those seen as the 'enemy', the unsmiling, overly serious, 'posh speaking' and inflexible regime that governs the school and is embodied in different ways by teachers and swots. This instance of 'low culture' contains, just as 'high culture' does, moral categories and refinements of judgement – who is worthy and unworthy of respect, who really deserves a lot of 'stick' and who less, and so on. Even in the most apparently unruly of behaviours there are certain codes of right and wrong conduct. In this case, 'good' conduct in the eyes of the lads is bad conduct in the eyes of the teachers, the representatives of the wider 'official' world as a whole.

A similar sense of the unwritten 'rules' you must follow in order effectively to break and disrupt official rules is given by the Irish writer Brendan Behan, who spent part of his teenage years in a borstal (youth prison). Here he describes how he subverted the authority of one of the warders:

> [He hands] me this dirty old bucket and hands me a piece of glass-paper, and says, 'Now, Bee-hann, you'll clean this bucket till it's like silvair'. 'I will', says I, 'in my ballocks – my big brown ones'. 'What is that you say, Bee-hann?' says he, gamming on not to get my meaning. 'I never saw a silver bucket in my fughing life' said I. So he lets on not to understand me, though he's shouting his head off … but by this time all the … kids are giggling and half-terrified but delighted to see me having this bastard on. 'I'll show you', says he, taking this piece of glasspaper in his hand, starting to rub this old bucket and squatting beside me in very comradely fashion. I have him bitched, ballocked and bewildered, for there is a system and a science in taking the piss out of a screw and I'm a well-trained young man at it.
>
> (Behan, 1990 [1958]: 366–367)

Behan notes that there are well-developed techniques for 'taking the piss' out of authority figures and he is well schooled in them. The effect on the other young in-mates is to get them giggling at how the warder has been bested by Behan, the giggling itself another degradation both of the warder personally and of the regime he represents.

It is the laughter of mockery and degradation that Bakhtin has in mind when he thought of how humour can be a weapon of the weak and oppressed. Moreover, the above passage describes the way the cheeky inmate spoke to the prison officer, using such crude expressions as 'in my ballocks – my big brown ones' and 'in my fughing life'. Behan's recollection therefore also indicates a central feature of the degrading sort of laughter Bakhtin is talking about. Anti-authoritarian humour is often very ribald and bawdy, disrespectful of the norms of 'civilized' society (see Chapter 1) by bringing taboo topics such as sex and excretion out into the open and laughing about them. The authority of social superiors can be mocked by, for example, telling 'dirty' jokes or making innuendos about them. For Bakhtin, such humour has its own 'aesthetics', its own specific ways of perceiving the world in general, and the nature of the human body in particular. The images invoked and lying behind such humour are of a human body that

> is not a closed, completed unit; it is unfinished, outgrows itself, transgresses its own limits. The stress is laid on those parts of the body which are open to the outside world ... the emphasis is on the apertures ... and offshoots: the open mouth, the genital organs, the breasts, the phallus, the potbelly and the nose [and the anus]. The body discloses its essence as a principle of growth which exceeds its own limits only in copulation, pregnancy, childbirth, the throes of death, eating, drinking, or defecation. This is the ever unfinished, ever creating body.
>
> (Bakhtin, 1984: 26)

The images of the body evoked by bawdy, anti-establishment humour are antithetical to what, in the Western tradition, Bakhtin (1984: 29) sees as 'high culture's' sense of the body, namely one that was 'strictly completed, finished, ... isolated, alone, fenced off from all other bodies'. The 'grotesque' body of ribald humour brings into social life that which social elites and their 'high culture' have sought to hide from sight, namely the 'material bodily stratum', those 'organic' aspects of human life that involve fucking, pissing, shitting, puking, menstruating and all the other ways in which the body can act in what high cultural norms define as 'disgusting' fashions.

Bakhtin's point here is that the foul and disgusting continually make an appearance in social life, despite the best attempts of authorities and regimes to regulate them. The grotesque need not just appear symbolically through the means of humour, it can also be embodied in certain people who are regarded by 'civilized' persons as utterly beyond the realms of cleanliness and respectability (Stallybrass and White, 1986). Here George Orwell describes how a church service was disrupted by members of that group that never ceases to receive the opprobrium of the polite classes in society, namely tramps and down-and-outs. They are in the church because attendance at the service is the price to be paid for the free meal they have just received:

The organ let out a few preliminary hoots and the service began. And instantly, as though at a signal, the tramps began to misbehave in the most outrageous way. One would not have thought such scenes possible in a church. All round the gallery men lolled in their pews, laughed, chattered, leaned over and flicked pellets of bread among the congregation. ... The tramps treated the service as a purely comic spectacle ... their behaviour passed all bounds. ... Sometimes somebody below would send up an indignant 'Hush!' but it made no impression. We had set ourselves to guy the service, and there was no stopping us. It was a queer, rather disgusting scene. ... A ring of dirty, hairy faces grinned down from the gallery, openly jeering.

(Orwell, 2003 [1933]: 196)

The loud and rude behaviour of the tramps and their grinning 'dirty, hairy faces' are a 'grotesque' irruption into the straight-laced world of the upright middle-class church-goers. Their interruption of the service, with their catcalls, their derisive laughing and their 'filthy' physical bodies and unkempt faces, can be seen as a low cultural invasion of bourgeois proprieties. They signify unruliness and disorder, a 'profane' interruption of the staid pieties of middle-class life. They are the chaos that threatens to blow apart orderly routines and conventional values. They are anarchy embodied.

Bakhtin and other 'populist' defenders of popular 'resistance' and 'creativity' rightly draw attention to how there is more to 'culture' than what is called 'high culture' alone. But equally well, we have to be careful not to celebrate uncritically the cultural powers of 'the people'. Orwell's example above goes on to note that far from being just an instance of healthy disregard for pomposity, the tramps' actions also had a rather dark side: 'What could a few women and old men do against a hundred hostile tramps? They were afraid of us, and we were frankly bullying them. It was our revenge upon them for having humiliated us by feeding us' (ibid.: 196). The tramps get their own back at the 'humiliation' of having to accept hand-outs; but in so doing they were treating with great disrespect those who may have gone out of their way to show them some kindness. There was a streak of (from one point of view) unnecessary nastiness in the tramps' display that we might not wish simply to celebrate as healthily anti-establishment. Likewise, the 'lads' in Willis's study had very pronounced xenophobic, racist and misogynistic attitudes. It is all very well for the relatively privileged onlooker on 'everyday life' to identify and celebrate the capacities and characteristics of 'low culture'; but 'low culture' just as much as 'high culture' contains its own ambivalences, hypocrisies and evils too. Neither 'art' nor 'grounded aesthetics' are beyond criticism or reproach.

CONCLUSION: CULTURAL CONFUSION?

In this chapter I have examined the (often controversial) ways in which 'high', 'popular' and 'low cultures' can be described, the ways in which they can impact on everyday life and the manners in which everyday life can impact upon them. Before I finish this chapter, I need to say a few words about how some people believe that the nature of these cultural 'areas' (if they are separate enough to call them that) are in the present day rapidly mutating, such that it is difficult to tell what is 'high' or 'low', or 'high' and 'popular' culture any more. Some allege (e.g. Twitchell, 1992) that in a 'post-modern' context (see Chapter 2) these distinctions have been abolished or that the borders between these areas have become more permeable than before. We could look for example at how, since the 1960s, images and issues from 'popular culture' (e.g. Andy Warhol's use of advertising for Campbell's soup in his art) have entered into the mainstream art world, such that there has been a blending of 'high' and 'low' elements, a situation often taken to be quintessentially 'post-modern' in nature. In the same vein, others (e.g. Peterson and Kern, 1996) point out that cultural distinctions are not today as clear cut as Bourdieu made out, that classes do not necessarily have 'their own' cultures any more, and that people on the whole are more culturally 'omnivorous', in that they blend and mix together different sorts of cultural forms in new and eclectic ways.

Clearly in a society where middle-class media types affect to have working-class cockney accents (thus being seen as 'mockneys') and when privately educated white schoolkids try to dress and speak like ghetto-raised black rappers, saying simply that 'high' culture on the one side and 'popular' and 'low' cultures on the other are wholly isolated from each other is a palpable absurdity. We might expect to find in a complex society equally complex mixings of cultural forms and forces. A focus on everyday life shows that it is pointless to characterize either 'high culture' as wholly above 'ordinary' concerns, or 'popular culture' as involving totally mindless consumption or 'low culture' as involving the wholly praiseworthy activities of downtrodden but plucky Robin Hoods. All simplistic depictions of these areas are revealed, through looking at their mundane operations, to be caricatures.

But I remain strongly convinced that it is equally easy to overstate the degree to which all these different sorts of culture have now apparently blended into a 'post-modern' whole. As long as a society is organized on the basis of classes, then class will continue to effect cultural forces and everyday life, although not necessarily in direct or immediately discernible ways. The middle-class rappers are still middle class as, generally, are the omnivores who like soap operas in the afternoon and opera at night. There is still not a great deal of omnivorousness going on outside the world of the relatively privileged. Tramps will continue to be able to act in 'low cultural' ways as long as homelessness remains a social issue. Likewise, as long as our society is organized into relatively – but not totally – separate spheres like the 'art world' and the 'mass media', the different 'levels' of culture will continue to exist in the future, although not necessarily in quite the ways we have been used to.

4

GLOBALIZATION, CULTURE AND EVERYDAY LIFE

INTRODUCTION

'Globalization' is a word that for most of us is almost inescapable these days. When jobs are lost in a particular town owing to a company relocating to another country, this is blamed on 'globalization'. When government officials tell us that spending on certain welfare services is going to be cut, we are told this is because the national economy is experiencing a downturn because of recession in the global economy, the latter being the driving force of globalization. When diverse groups of people take to the streets to protest against environmental degradation, sweat-shop labour, Third World debt and a host of other issues, they see themselves as standing up against the forces of globalization. And when we are told that Britain and other Western countries are becoming ever more like the United States, this is often blamed on globalization too. On a more positive note, when we are also told that Britain and other countries are becoming evermore 'multicultural' and our cultural tastes evermore 'cosmopolitan', this is also alleged to be due to globalization, to the way that national cultures are being opened up and made more diverse and more tolerant and celebratory of 'others' owing to the globalization of cultural life.

In this chapter I will look at the ways in which the effects of 'globalization' on cultural forms and everyday practices can be thought about. I will examine the various means by which 'globalization' may be implicated in the ways we think and act on a daily basis, and whether or not it is having significant effects on the cultural forces that shape our everyday lives. The central controversy we will deal with is whether 'globalization' makes the cultural aspects of daily life more homogeneous or heterogeneous, that is whether different parts of the world are all becoming more culturally 'alike' or whether globalizing forces actually cultivate new and more trends towards cultural differentiation. How these competing trends can influence ordinary practices will be the theme running throughout the chapter.

I will first of all examine different understandings of the word 'globalization', and we will see that it is better to understand it not as referring to a single and uniform mega-process but to a whole series of diverse, sometimes complementary, but in other ways potentially contradictory, trends and forces that are fully or partially 'world-wide' in scale and ramifications. I will then turn to examine the view that a Western- and especially American-dominated culture has arisen which threatens to transform and destroy more 'traditional' and 'local' cultural practices. Next I will look at criticisms of that view, which hold that such 'local' cultural activities remain buoyant in the face of, in fact perhaps are revitalized by, the forces of globalization. I will then look at the possibility that cultural forms and practices are becoming ever more 'hybrid' in nature, such that the contemporary cultural situation in a country like Britain could be said to be thoroughly diverse in nature. I will outline the possibility that such mixings and matchings of cultural forms and forces are not just recent developments but have been present in many parts of the world for centuries. I will then look at these issues, and their ramifications for how everyday activities are structured, by examining a case study, that of transnational trends in food. I will conclude by considering how 'cosmopolitan' or otherwise everyday life has become under conditions of globalization.

COMPREHENDING GLOBALIZATION

'Globalization' is a word that has a number of different, potentially contradictory, meanings. In popular discourse, it has come to have primarily economic meanings. Both the supporters of 'global capitalism', in the form of transnational corporations and big business, and its critics, tend towards the view that 'globalization' is a fundamentally economic phenomenon, involving the creation of world-spanning free markets and the global reach of capitalist systems of production and consumption. Whether one believes that global capitalism brings with it jobs, opportunities, increasing wealth and higher standards of living, or whether one thinks that it leaves in its wake a trail of social and environmental disaster, the shared belief among both business executives and 'anti-globalization' protesters is that globalization is in essence a phenomenon of multinational capitalism.

Contemporary popular discourse thus follows, albeit mostly unintentionally, the views of Marx and Engels, when in the middle of the nineteenth century they wrote in the 'Manifesto of the Communist Party' (1983 [1848]: 38) that 'the need of a constantly expanding market for its products chases the bourgeoisie over the whole surface of the globe'. For a present-day analyst of global capitalism such as Thomas Friedman (1999: 7–8), economically defined globalization involves

> the inexorable integration of markets, nation-states, and technologies to a degree never witnessed before ... in a way that is enabling individuals, corporations and nation-states to reach around the world farther, faster, deeper and cheaper than ever before. ... [The end result of these processes is] the spread of free-market capitalism to virtually every country in the world.

If capitalist markets are now not just *inter*national but in fact *trans*national in scope, this would seem to have certain severe repercussions for the degree to which national governments remain in control of their economic – and other – affairs. A state with unquestioned control over its own 'national' territory is an innovation of the West in the early modern period. Over the last several hundred years, individual states have (at least in theory) had the power to run affairs within their own borders. According to some observers, what economic globalization does is to undermine the power of the state within its own territory. If transnational corporations can pick and choose which countries to situate their business within, if capital and resources are geographically mobile, if capitalist markets stretch all across the world with the result that all national economies are bound up with each other, then it would

seem to be the case that the capacity of the state to control its own economic affairs is undermined, perhaps seriously so (Held and McGrew,
2000).

The degree to which states increasingly lack economic power – and
thus other sorts of power too – within the present-day global system
remains a contested issue, with some claiming the day of the nation-
state is now well and truly over and others arguing that claims as to the
demise of the state are very overstated. What most would agree on,
however, is that individual states today find themselves operating
within a series of constraints that are probably more developed than was
the case hitherto – states have to work within an environment where
they are hemmed in not just by the machinations of global corporations,
but also by international law, international bodies like the United
Nations and the World Trade Organization, inter-state bodies like the
European Union and global-level pressure groups like Amnesty
International and Greenpeace. The upshot of all this is that, at the very
least, states are more constrained as institutional actors in the present
day than they may have ever been before (Hardt and Negri, 2000).

Now that I have examined economically defined globalization and its
apparent political ramifications, I will turn to consider other views of
globalization which see within it social and cultural elements too. In
terms of social factors, Giddens (1990: 64) views globalization as
involving 'the intensification of worldwide social relations which link
distant localities in such a way that local happenings are shaped by
events occurring many miles away and vice versa'. In other words, what
happens in one society can have effects in a number of others, often in
unexpected ways, indicating that most or all national societies are now
connected with each other in increasingly complex ways. For Martin
Albrow (1996: 88), globalization in part means a situation where
'global practices and so on exercise an increasing influence over people's
lives', where 'global practices' could mean various things, from a big
corporation closing down a factory in one country and moving it to
another where costs are lower, to a non-governmental organization such
as Friends of the Earth campaigning in national or local media. The central point is that under conditions of globalization, what happens *here* is
influenced not just by what happens *there* but in a whole series of *theres*.

In a similar vein, David Held *et al.* (1999: 16) see globalization as
involving transformations 'in the spatial organization of social relations

and transactions – assessed in terms of their extensity, intensity, velocity and impact – generating transcontinental or inter-regional flows and networks of activity'. What in part they mean by this is that social relationships are no longer primarily tied to 'local' areas and within the boundaries of states. The people you work and do business with, the friends you have, the acquaintances you know – all could be located in geographically distant locales. A person's relationships and forms of interaction become increasingly unconstrained by geography and are no longer necessarily 'local' or 'national' in nature.

Giddens (1990) also highlights the changing nature of time and space under globalizing conditions. When a jet aircraft can transport you a vast geographical distance from a society on one side of the world to another on the other side in a fraction of the time it used to take, say, by boat, then the connections that used to hold between time and space are shattered and new connections are put in place. In the nineteenth century, it took several weeks to travel by ship from Britain to the United States, whereas nowadays by aircraft it only takes a matter of hours. This alteration in time and space can changes people's conceptions of the nature of their social relations. If one's relatives live four weeks away by boat, then they will seem far way, but if they are only six hours away by aircraft, they might not seem so very far away at all.

In this light, Malcolm Waters (1995: 3) defines globalization as a 'social process in which the constraints of geography on social and cultural arrangements recede and in which people become increasingly aware that they are receding'. This definition usefully highlights the possibility that globalization is not just about the 'world becoming smaller' but that people's actions and beliefs are affected and changed precisely because they believe that is indeed the case.

This takes us towards the cultural aspects of globalization, in so far as culture involves how particular groups of people think and feel about the world around them. Roland Robertson (1992: 8) insists that globalization involves not just material changes as to how people live – that is, changes in economic, political and social circumstances – but also changes in how they think, both in general and about those circumstances themselves. Globalization is therefore to be seen as 'the compression of the world and the intensification of consciousness of the world as a whole'. Concomitant with economic, political and social aspects of globalization, there is also a key cultural development, namely 'globality', which is comprised of forms of consciousness and ways of thinking which regard the whole earth as 'one place' (Beck, 2000). Feelings of globality are dramatized in, for example, self-consciously 'global' affairs as the Olympics, Live Aid and the aptly named soccer World Cup. Such 'global' imaginings come more and more to shape how we think, feel and respond to things; we come to see our individual lives as being thoroughly connected to and dependent on events and affairs that encompass everyone and everything on the planet.

CULTURE AND THE GLOBAL

We saw above that most analysts of globalization concur that in the present day, what happens in one particular place is influenced by what happens in a whole series of other places. This situation has important ramifications for how we comprehend the forces that shape everyday life. According to a number of observers, we should not see these forces as being purely 'local' in scale any more – that is, as formed and operating within purely 'local' communities or within the boundaries of particular nation-states. We can no longer understand how our lives are formed solely in terms of local-level phenomena or national-level affiliations, because both the 'local' and the 'national' are nowadays bound up with wider, more 'global' phenomena and forces (Robertson, 1992: 37). As Beck (2000: 47) phrases the point, 'local cultures can no longer be justified, shaped and renewed in seclusion from the rest of the world'. Instead of looking at how everyday life is lived within a particular nationally based society – for example, France, Canada, Malta – we must look instead at how people who live within the borders of a particular state are affected by, respond to and themselves help to create forces that are transnational in nature. Our focus should move away from only conceiving of human life in terms of how it is affected by national 'societies', towards augmenting that view with comprehension of how everyday activities are influenced by, and are part of, 'global networks and flows' (Urry, 2000).

This also means that, as Robertson (1992: 112) puts it, it is not a good idea to 'carry into the study of globalization the kind of view of culture that we inherit from the conventional analysis of the national society'. It is no longer adequate just to look at 'British culture', 'German culture' and so on. Instead, what we must do is to consider the ways in which 'the interconnectedness of the world, by way of interactions, exchanges and related developments, affect[s] ... the organization of culture' (Hannerz, 1996: 7). What this means more concretely is that we have to look at how culture is created, shaped, reworked and contested within and across national borders, examining, for example, the relations that pertain between cultural centres (e.g. Hollywood) and peripheries (e.g. Third World countries) (Hannerz, 1989).

An important aspect of the 'globalization of culture' is 'deterritorialization' – the ways in which global-level forces can diminish the significance of social and geographical location in the creation and experience of cultural phenomena (Garcia-Canclini, 1995). What we have to examine are the means by which culture is 'lifted out' of its traditional 'anchoring' in particular locales. For example, Mexican food originates in, and reflects the agricultural production of, a particular part of Central America. But through the spread of fast-food restaurants like Taco Bell, a version of Mexican food has become a mainstay of North American eating habits. Mexican food has been decoupled from its place of origin to become part of a more 'global' lexicon of tastes in food. Our cultural experiences are no longer as rooted as they were in the places we happen to live. The cultural possibilities on offer in a particular locale are no longer wholly or mostly 'traditional' to that locale. Under globalizing conditions, the local (or what we think of as the local) is no longer the main determining factor in what the culture of a particular place involves. Cultural phenomena can be transplanted and take root in places many thousands of miles from where they originated. Widespread cultural transplantation (where 'widespread' means both ubiquity and movement over great geographical distances) is a key feature of a globalizing world.

CULTURAL IMPERIALISM, AMERICANIZATION AND 'GLOBAL CULTURE'

Just as we saw in Chapter 3 that debates over 'high culture' and 'popular culture' are hugely contentious and involve an array of different critical opinions, so too are the evaluations of the effects of globalization on cultural affairs very controversial.

On the one hand, there are those who regard globalization as having a very positive effect on cultural contexts around the world. For example, one might see the important role Western media organizations play in creating and distributing a great deal of the world's televisual and cinematic entertainment as a great boon for the world as a whole. The owner of the cable and satellite news channel CNN, Ted Turner, famously declared that 'with CNN, information circulates throughout the world, and no-one wants to look like an idiot. So they make peace, because that's smart' (Mattelart, 2000: 95). His point was that CNN's potentially all-encompassing and 'global' news coverage of world affairs would encourage peaceful relations between states, because the 'whole world' could see if a particular regime was acting unreasonably or dangerously; the threat of being condemned in the eyes of global public opinion would be enough to force potentially rogue states to give up their eccentric policies.

Certainly in light of events like Saddam Hussein's defiance of 'world opinion' – or Western-influenced world opinion, depending on your point of view – over weapons inspections and suchlike, and the war that ensued as a result, Turner's comments seem rather naive. But a more plausible argument is that the development of communication media like satellite TV, digital radio and the Internet are great boons for freedom of information and human rights. This is because they can transcend national borders. People living within a particular state's territory can at least potentially receive information from outside the borders of that country, even if the authorities do not wish to them to have access to such information. If a regime is abusive of human rights, and this fact is never mentioned in the official national media, news of this state of affairs can still leak out among the population if they have access to media that broadcast from another country. While repressive national states would seek to control and deny that access, the point still remains: it is nowadays probably more difficult than ever before for states to control what information flows into their territory, a situation that could have unpredictable effects on the population within.

On the other hand, there is no shortage of critics of the globalization of the mass media. Far from being means of universal information flow and political liberation, the Western mass media companies can be seen as Trojan horses of Western capitalistic and consumerist values, spreading ideas and encouraging ways of life which undermine 'local' cultures, in that these are 'battered out of existence by the indiscriminate dumping of large quantities of slick commercial media products, mainly from the United States' (Tunstall, 1977: 57). The (primarily American) mass media are on this view purveyors of 'cultural imperialism', involved in the imposition of the set of values of one country or region (the United States, the 'West') onto another country or region.

In specifically media industry terms, it is alleged that the 'mass culture' (see Chapter 3) of Hollywood spreads all across the world, contaminating and defacing local cultures as it goes. An early expression of this sort of view was offered by the American cultural critic Clement Greenberg (1986 [1939]: 13–14), writing in the late 1930s:

> Kitsch [i.e. manufactured mass culture] has not been confined to the cities in which it was born, but has flowed out over the countryside, wiping out folk culture. Nor has it shown any regard for geographical and national-cultural boundaries. Another mass product of Western industrialism, it has gone on a triumphal tour of the world, crowding out and defacing native cultures in one ... country after another, so that it is now by way of becoming a universal culture, the first universal culture ever. ... Today the native of China, no less than the South American Indian, the Hindu, no less than the Polynesian, have come to prefer to the products of their native art, magazine covers ... and calendar girls.

The argument can easily be updated. The global exportation by Western media corporations of pop idols like Britney Spears, of films with the likes of Bruce Willis, and of TV programmes like *Friends*, can be seen as pushing to the peripheries of national and local media cultures more indigenous products, made in the countries of transmission.

The notion of cultural imperialism need not only apply to cultural transfers and transplantations between the 'West' and the rest of the world. It can also apply to unequal cultural relationships between the United States and other Western nations. This has been a fear of certain social groups in Britain since the time of Matthew Arnold in the mid-nineteenth century (see Chapter 3). The trepidation has involved the possibility that authentically 'British' (or more narrowly, 'English') culture would be overwhelmed by American ideas, attitudes and ways of doing things. In a famous description from the 1950s of the then-popular 'milk bars' where teenagers would gather to listen to rock 'n' roll records on the jukebox, Richard Hoggart (1962 [1957]: 248) bemoaned what he took to be the fabricated nature of American-influenced youth culture, comparing it unfavourably with the more 'traditional' local pub:

> Compared even with the pub around the corner, this is all a peculiarly thin and pallid form of dissipation, a sort of spiritual dry-rot amid the odour of boiled milk. Many of the customers – their clothes, their hair-styles, their facial expressions all indicate – are living to a large extent in a myth world compounded of a few simple elements which they take to be those of American life.

From this point of view, imported American culture was seeping slowly but surely into the fabric of English cultural life. The tawdry American or American-style cultural products increasingly enjoyed by working-class English people – cheap thrillers and cowboy novels, detective shows on TV – were subverting and destroying from within the traditional cultural pursuits of the working class – beer and skittles, darts, sing-a-longs in the local pub, pigeon-fancying, and so on. American mass culture was characterized by 'an endless flux of the undistinguished and the valueless' (ibid.: 194).

Hoggart's example and the language in which he expresses it may seem rather dated. But an evaluation of the cultural depredations effected by American popular culture on the ways of life of other countries continues to be a major theme today. In France, for example, the fast-food chain McDonald's is taken as a symbol of an American takeover of 'traditional' French folkways, most notably in that most sensitive of areas, cuisine. The farmer Jose Bove, who famously bulldozed a branch of McDonald's in protest at what he saw as the degradation of French culture in general and food culture in particular, became a popular hero in France (at least according to the French press), because of his apparently heroic stance against creeping Americanization (Bove *et al.*, 2002).

The apparent 'triumph' of American culture, in Europe and in other places, is today generally regarded as involving the global ubiquity of certain brands and labels. Apart from McDonald's, other brands recognizable by people in most parts of the world today include Coca-Cola, Pepsi, Disney, Levis and Nike. Some European-based brands, like Benetton and Nokia, are also internationally present. The great presence of these labels, and the ideas they connote, around the world, is certainly a key cultural feature of the early twenty-first century. As Beck (2000: 42) puts it, in 'the villages of Lower Bavaria, just as in Calcutta, Singapore or the "favelas" of Rio de Janeiro, people watch Dallas on TV, wear blue jeans and smoke Marlboro'. Consequently, it is possible to view this collection of symbols, products and ideas as the constituent elements of a 'new world culture' (Cvetkovich and Kellner, 1997: 7), the 'first universal culture ever' that Greenberg spoke about above. Is it possible that the first ever truly 'global culture' is the one characterized by Francis Fukuyama (1992) in his famous prognostication as to the 'end of history', namely a culture made up of the twin Western values of individualism and consumerism?

A further interesting feature of what some might want to call 'global culture' is its – perhaps peculiarly 'Western' – sense of impersonality and reproducibility. The buildings in modern business districts of large cities in different parts of the world are all characterized by a certain style of impersonal modernist architecture, and contain within them the same sorts of businesses with the same sorts of office decor, the same sorts of hotels, and the same sorts of malls with 'upscale' shops. It is sometimes difficult to tell when one is inside one of these locales where in the world one is, except if a rather tacky or self-conscious display of 'local culture' is on display in the atrium or lobby, to remind one of the 'authentic' place one is otherwise being so carefully protected from. The same is true of places such as airline departure lounges and shuttle trains to and from airports. The way they look makes them seem infinitely placeable in almost any part of the world, from Buenos Aires to Belfast. They are exemplars of what Augé (1995) calls 'non-places', globalized spaces within particular places which deny and hide the particularities of the place they are surrounded by. If 'global culture' exists, it manifests itself most clearly in such decontextualized and deterritorialized locales as the international hotel conference suite and restaurant, and the duty-free stores at airports. Through these places the global business elite can move comfortably, barely registering the differences between the countries they pass through.

LOCAL RESPONSES

Thus far, I have emphasized how both the cultural products that people watch, read and hear, and the cultural contexts in which they live more generally, can be seen as having been transformed by the onset of the globalization of culture. We can see 'global culture' as being a primarily Western/American and consumerist entity, which erodes local cultural particularities and specificities. On an extreme version of this view, daily life in many parts of the world is being restructured along the lines of the typical American shopping mall and cinema arcade. Clearly there are elements of truth in this view. One only has to go to a multiplex cinema to see how patterned it is on an American model – most of the films are from Hollywood, the foods offered are snacks like hot-dogs, popcorn and cola which are standardized on American lines, and in some ways if you are standing in the ticket queue the surroundings and general ambiance are exactly like those in thousands of similar places across North America.

Yet even in this apparently most 'American' of 'non-spaces', local cultural forces are at work. The accents of the people wearing the standardized uniforms of the fast-food outlets betray the fact that you are in Manchester, not Muncie, Indiana. With the local accents come more local attitudes and concerns, such as how the local football team are currently doing or what nightclubs are currently the places to go and which are to be avoided. Even if the people in those clubs are listening to music that is listened to all over the world, it is still unlikely that local concerns will ever be completely obliterated by 'globalizing' cultural tendencies.

As Tomlinson (1997) notes, ideas as to 'cultural imperialism' can be accused of greatly oversimplifying both the nature of 'global culture' and its alleged effects on local circumstances. These latter are regarded too romantically as originally 'untouched' by the contaminating forces of Western culture, when they are themselves often the products of hundreds of years of cultural interpenetration and mixing (as we will see further below). Furthermore, as Held and McGrew (2000) argue, it is not simply the case that American cultural products have totally squeezed out 'indigenous' TV programmes, films, music, books, and so on. One need only look at the predominance of Bollywood films in the Indian subcontinent and of locally made films in Hong Kong to realize that a simple view of the United States as a cultural centre dominating cultural peripheries is too crude a way of looking at what is a more complicated situation of cross-border traffic in entertainments. It remains the case that 'national institutions continue in many states to have a central impact on public life; national television and radio broadcasting continues to enjoy substantial audiences; the organization of the press and news coverage retains strong national roots' (ibid.: 16). We are not yet at the stage where the likes of CNN and Rupert Murdoch's media empire thoroughly control national media cultures as diverse as those of Indonesia and Ireland.

It is partly on this basis that Held and McGrew dispute the existence of a 'global culture' at all. There is no such thing as there is not spread across the world today a universal 'culture' in any deep sense of the word, a 'culture' which would involve a 'common pool of memories ... [a] common global way of thinking; and ... [a] 'universal history' in and through which people can unite' (ibid.). Instead, what we have today is arguably a series of different ethnically and religiously based value systems engaged in a series of, at best, uneasy relationships, and, at worst, violent confrontations (Huntington, 1998). Indeed, in a world where religious and nationalist fundamentalisms are now ever present, it might be better to see Western capitalist culture, with its brands and logos, as but one element of a wider cultural configuration, made up of both 'McWorld' on the one side and 'Jihad' on the other. Following the logic of Benjamin Barber's (1992) argument in this direction, it is in many ways the socio-cultural and socio-economic nexus of 'global consumer capitalism' which ironically has helped to engender virulent responses to itself, most explosively dramatized in the events of 11 September 2001. If a global consumerism helps to create its own 'others', forms of religious and ethnic–nationalist zealotry which loathe all they think it stands for, then we are very far from being within an overarching 'world culture' where everyone feels affinity with everyone else. It may well be the case that one of the paradoxes of globalization processes is that they tend to throw up not only trends towards cultural homogenization but also vigorous responses to and resistances to that homogenization. Even in the West, as the vociferous presence of the 'anti-globalization' movements makes clear, there is no uniformity as to how people make sense of and respond to the supposed triumph of global consumerism.

It is all very well to theorize about the effects of global culture indus-tries on local environments, but, just as we saw in Chapter 3 in terms of audience responses to media products, how people respond to films, TV, music and other cultural forms made for popular consumption is a mat-ter for empirical investigation, rather than speculation and unfounded assertion. Assuming that American-made films and TV programmes and global brands like Nike and Coke completely 'destroy' local cul-tures unintentionally reproduces a view of things that advertising and media executives would love to be the case. As David Howes (1996: 7) puts it, 'the world as seen through the window of the corporate board-room ... may well look like a single place ... but ... there is rather more going on "out there" ' than such an outlook can discern.

On entering another cultural context, the meaning of a particular cultural product may change from the significance it had, or was intended to have, in its original place of production (Axford, 1995). Indeed, it may be the very 'Westernness' of a film or TV programme that provokes its reinterpretation in specific local contexts; if some-thing seems very alien, viewers can make sense of it by reinterpreting it in light of the cultural codes they are familiar with. No TV pro-gramme seems to embody the crass materialism of Reagan's America than *Dallas*. Yet, as Elihu Katz and Tamar Liebes (1985) argued in their study of more reactions to the programme amongst different social groups in Israel, the cultural values of the group in question impinged greatly upon individuals' responses to the show. Recently arrived immigrants from Russia took the film not as a celebration of capitalist society but as a critique of it, and Arab groups saw in it a warning against the degenerative effects of Western culture. In a simi-lar vein, Daniel Miller (1992) found that the reception in Trinidad of the US daytime soap opera *The Young and the Restless* involved under-standing the programme through a mesh of local cultural concerns, Trinidadians relating the programme to situations in their own day-to-day lives.

Such points apply not only in places outside the West but in the West itself. It would be a great mistake to assert that there is such a thing as a wholly homogeneous 'Western culture', driven by the con-sumer products made by large corporations, which has blanket coverage over every sector of Western societies. The last are arguably too large, too complex and too internally diverse and fractured to allow a situation where such a culture was totally dominant, even if its influences are indeed still powerful in certain senses. As Saskia Sassen (1998: xxxi) puts it:

> The large Western city of today concentrates diversity. Its spaces are inscribed with the dominant corporate culture, but also with a multiplicity of other cultures and identities. The slippage is evident: the dominant culture can encompass only part of the city. And while corporate power inscribes these cultures and identifies them with 'otherness' thereby devaluing them, they are present everywhere.

Wherever one happens to be in the world, even in the capitalist epicentres like New York and London, it seems unlikely one would ever encounter a situation where corporate consumerist culture was fully and unproblematically hegemonic. It may well be a fact of human life that even in the most totalitarian of contexts, alternative voices and ideas will emerge which are antithetical to the dominant power order (as we saw de Certeau and Bakhtin argue in Chapter 3). Thus instead of thinking that the effect of 'global' or 'American' culture on local cultural contexts is one characterized by total erasure of the latter, it might be better to regard such contexts as involving *mélanges* of different cultural forms, ranging from the most apparently 'global' such as advertising hoardings for Coca-Cola to the most apparently local and regional, such as paraphernalia to do with local religious cults and icons (Classen, 1996). Moreover, the mere presence of 'foreign' influences need not *necessarily* have much of an effect on everyday forms of thought and action. As Tomlinson (1997: 87) argues:

> In everyday activities like working, eating or shopping, people are likely to be concerned with their immediate needs – their state of health, their family and personal relations, their finances and so on. In these circumstances the cultural significance of working for a multinational, eating lunch at McDonalds, shopping for Levis, is unlikely to be interpreted as a threat to national identity, but how these mesh with the meaningful realm of the private: McDonalds as convenient for the children's birthday party; jeans as a dress code for leisure-time activities.

In other words, in certain circumstances, everyday life can indeed be revolutionized by 'outside' and 'global' influences, but in other circumstances, mundane activities and ways of thinking might remain relatively impervious to such things. People might be eating in McDonald's but this does not necessarily mean that they have all become 'American' or 'Western' in their thoughts, attitudes and lifestyles (even assuming that it was totally clear and unambiguous what 'American-ness' or 'Western-ness' meant). The question of the effects wrought by changing cultural patterns and influences is an empirical one that can only be investigated by finding out what actually goes on 'on the ground', rather than being decided beforehand in the seminar room or the armchair.

ENDLESS MULTIPLICITY?

The general point here is that rather than being swept away by the onslaught of 'global culture', most people's cultural experience today can be seen as a complex mixture of interactions between the 'local' and the 'global' (Cvetkovich and Kellner, 1997). Sometimes, in certain contexts and in certain ways, the 'global' may be more predominant (e.g. the eating habits of a particular place shift massively in a short space of time towards American-style fast food); at other times and in other contexts, the 'local' may be the more dominant feature of people's experience (e.g. the fast-food culture of a place remains primarily based around the ingredients and tastes of 'traditional' and 'local' street-food). Sometimes the interpenetration of the 'local' and the 'global' can produce new forms of specifically 'local' culture, while at other times distinctive new combinations of local and global can be created.

Such new combinations can be described variously as 'hybrid' or 'creole'. Processes of hybridization and creolization involve the interweaving of hitherto separate – or relatively separate – cultural patterns, ideas, tastes, styles and attitudes (Werbner, 1997; Bhabha, 1994). Specific 'hybrid' products can emerge in local contexts, while more generic 'global culture' itself can be seen as a hybridized coming together of hitherto relatively discrete cultural traditions. An aesthetic of mixing and mingling, whereby, for example, Western traditions are fused with Asian and African influences, could be seen as the quintessence of 'global culture', a rather different understanding of the latter term than one which emphasizes its purely Western and corporate consumerist roots (Pieterse, 1995).

A focus on 'hybrid' and 'creole' cultures compels us to look at how different cultural worlds can come together – or deliberately be brought together by certain people – and then mesh, combine and mutate, producing novel forms and styles. But it would be misleading simply to think that 'in the past' different ethnically or geographically based cultural traditions were wholly separate from each other, whereas 'now' in a globalizing world context they have suddenly collided together. There is some truth in this, of course, but it has been the case that throughout human history, different groups have encountered each other, in the process learning new ways of thinking and doing things. Often this has been through the means of warfare, conquest and empire-building, but even violent clashes between different groups do not necessarily imply that the culture of the 'losers' gets totally wiped out by the culture of the 'winners'.

Certainly this was pretty much the case in terms of the European colonization of North America, where native American culture was almost totally displaced by the invaders. But even in the equally notorious case of the Spanish conquest of South America in the 1500s, when the life conditions of indigenous civilizations were severely disrupted by the activities of the conquistadors, the flame of 'local culture' was not entirely extinguished, but rather in some cases took on new, rather unexpected forms. Although the Spanish 'converted' the natives to Christianity, local religions survived by adapting to and taking on the external form of Christianity. Local religious cults of saints and saints days, for example, were in fact survivals of pre-conquest religious beliefs, covered with a layer of Christian iconography (de Certeau, 1984). The same is true of the relationship between pagan beliefs and Christian rituals in Europe itself, the site of an apparently homogeneously 'Christian' culture. For example, the practice of having a Christmas tree in one's home has been yoked to a Christian celebration, but the roots of the practice of having a tree decorated with light in or near one's abode during mid-winter lie in the pagan practices of the Germanic peoples of northern Europe. Despite the best attempts of ruling elites, be they religious or political, the hybridization of culture can still occur and can, on occasion, usurp the authority of the dominant culture in tacit and subterranean ways.

A situation of pervasive cultural hybridity could indeed be argued to be the primal cultural condition of those parts of the world that for a very long time have had relatively regularized trading links with each other. Before the age of European world-wide expansion from the sixteenth century onwards, the Americas and Australasia were not in contact with Europe, Asia and Africa. However, as the American anthropologist Alfred Kroeber (1948) has argued, for thousands of years there have been culture contacts between different groups living in the landmass from Ireland in the west, to Japan in the east, and Africa above the Sahara to the south.

In fact Kroeber (1945) claims that there was such a great deal of cultural traffic between different regions in this area that one can talk to some degree about a common 'Eurasian culture', albeit one that possessed a great deal of local colouring. Kroeber suggests a number of cultural phenomena which arose in one part of that area and then spread to many other parts of it. For example, astrology was first invented several thousand years ago in Mesopotamia (modern Iraq), spread westwards to Egypt, and from there into ancient Greek and Roman civilization, and then finally onwards to the Islamic world and medieval Western Europe. Astrology also moved eastwards, going from Mesopotamia on through India and ending up in Bali. In a similar fashion, chess started in India, moved westwards to Persia and Turkey, at which point it was taken up by the Arabs and passed by them on to the Europeans. It also spread northwards and eastwards to Mongolia, Tibet and Indonesia. In both the cases of astrology and chess, as they moved from one area to the next they retained certain of their original characteristics, but they also gained particular local colourings and flavourings, taking up ideas, styles and attitudes from the locales that they took root in.

GLOBALIZATION IN ACTION: GLOBAL CUISINE

Given the above, it would seem to be the case that some sort of 'hybridity' has been a part of human life in Eurasia for millennia, and thus is not a totally novel aspect of people's cultural existences confined to the later twentieth century and beyond. But it is also the case that hybridization processes in the present day happen at a much faster rate, involve greater numbers of 'different' and more geographically dispersed cultures, and are more self-consciously enacted and thought about by people than ever was the case before.

The long history of 'hybridity', coupled with its greater accentuation and presence in the world in the present day, can be shown through a particular example, that of food cultures. In one way, food has not particularly been subject to hybridization processes for long tracts of human history, as people have simply had to eat food that was readily available in their immediate surroundings. Particular ethnically and regionally based peasant cuisines have as their ingredients foodstuffs that are generally readily available in the particular environment a given social group lives within. For example, the Scottish dish of haggis is 'traditional' precisely because it is made up of ingredients – oatmeal and sheep's innards – which were relatively easily available to the pre-modern Scottish peasantry, both in terms of growing and rearing conditions and in terms of monetary cost.

But under certain social, political and economic conditions, all this can change. Certain groups, especially elite groups, can come to have access to ingredients and dishes that come from further afield than the immediate local area. For example, if you live in a great city at the heart of an empire, then all the goods that come in from far-flung regions of that empire can be yours if you have sufficient spending power. At the height of the Roman Empire, for example, goods flooded into Rome from as far away as Scotland and China (Robertson and Inglis, 2004). This meant that the variety of foods available was greatly expanded over the rather modest range available to Romans in earlier centuries. Moreover, new recipes and people to cook them appeared from far-off parts of the empire, changing the taste-buds of the Roman elite quite dramatically. A contemporary author here describes how Roman gourmets increasingly demanded that there be brought

> from all regions everything, known or unknown, to tempt their fastidious palate[s]: food, which their stomach, worn out with delicacies, can scarcely retain, is brought from the most distant ocean ... they do not even deign to digest the banquets which they ransack the globe to obtain ... they wander through all countries, cross the seas and excite at a great cost the hunger which they might allay at a small one.
>
> (Seneca, 1889: 334–335)

Roman authors identified as a common practice among elites the mixing and matching of different culinary cultures, and the creation of hybrid dishes based on ingredients from different national larders. Quaint, unfamiliar ingredients from foreign lands were sought by wealthy Romans and chefs were happy to indulge in what culinary traditionalists saw as evermore bizarre mixings of flavours and textures from across the world. This shows that hybridization in food is not solely a modern innovation.

Indeed, many other historical examples of tendencies towards the mixing together of foods from different traditions and places can be found. Once one starts investigating the history of 'traditional' 'national' food cultures, one begins to see to what a great degree these are not just made up of ingredients that have been available locally since time immemorial. They are often in the present day as much constituted of ingredients that originated from other places, but which have been adopted into the national food repertoire. Over time, the foreign origins of these foods become forgotten and they come to seem as if they have been part of the national larder for ever. One important factor that has to be taken into account here is the revolution in the availability of different food products that has occurred over the last 500 years or so, ever since the European 'discovery' of the Americas. Many of the ingredients and tastes we take for granted today in fact originated in South America and were wholly unknown in Europe before European settlers and conquerors brought them back to their mother countries. Without the expansion of the Spanish Empire throughout the sixteenth century, we would not today be familiar with the tastes of either chocolate or peanuts, crops that are now grown in other parts of the world but which were once available in the Americas only. Even more peculiar is the thought that the potato would probably not play such an important role in our food culture if it had not been brought back from South America by the means of European conquest (Fernandez-Armesto, 2001).

To a certain extent, national food cultures are made possible by a collective forgetting of the exotic origins of certain ingredients. For example, nothing seems more essentially Italian than the tomato, but it came from the Americas, along with gnocchi (made from potatoes) and polenta (made from maize, another South American staple). In the same vein, we associate chillies with the cooking of India and certain Far Eastern countries, yet they too are indigenous to South America. A converse process of transatlantic movement in foodstuffs happened as well – from Europe and Africa to the Americas and the Caribbean came crops such as rice and bananas, and animals such as beef cattle. Nothing sounds more Mexican than chilli-con-carne but if it involves either beef or rice, it is using ingredients that came to the Americas only in the last few hundred years (Fernandez-Armesto, 2001).

As we saw in the case of ancient Rome, it is perhaps the case that empires above all are the means by which the ways people eat have been transformed in more hybrid directions. An empire can not only move around food products throughout its territory, encouraging their planting or rearing in places they were previously unknown, but also shift around vast numbers of people to diverse places within its sphere of control or influence. The central reason why there are Indian and Chinese restaurants in practically every part of Britain, no matter how remote, is the migration of large numbers of people to this country from the former British colonies of India, Pakistan, Bangladesh and Hong Kong. These people have brought with them their food cultures and have drawn upon these to earn a livelihood in their new homeland. To a large extent, therefore, it is as a legacy of the British Empire – a now largely defunct enterprise – that Britain in the present day has embraced the curry and the spare rib as central parts of its culinary repertoire. The unintended effect of British imperialism has been seriously to change, over a relatively short period, the ideas the British have of what they wish to put in their mouths. The popularity of Indonesian food in Holland, and Vietnamese and North African cuisine in France, attests to the same process of culinary mixing – the cuisines of those who were colonized come to figure as major factors in the taste cultures of the colonizers and their ancestors.

It is the post-colonial situation in which we live that has bred the vastly diverse range of taste possibilities that today make up culinary culture in Western (and other) societies. Different ingredients, peoples, food styles and attitudes have come together and merge in ever new configurations and constellations. There is therefore much more to the globalization of food cultures than merely the ubiquity of McDonald's and Kentucky Fried Chicken. Allison James (1996) has provided a useful mapping out of this terrain in contemporary Britain.

In the first place, there is the *mass production of 'foreign' food*. In the 1950s, the food writer Elizabeth David encountered great resistance to her attempts to introduce 'Mediterranean' textures and flavours into the domestic repertoire of British cookery. This was perhaps unsurprising as at the time olive oil was still available only in chemists and diagnosed as a treatment for various ailments! Yet now southern Italian, southern French, Spanish and Greek ingredients and recipes are available in every supermarket. As the large supermarket chains from the 1960s onwards both reflected and themselves cultivated changing public attitudes towards food, more and more items that had previously been regarded as queer and exotic became indigenized and familiar. Nothing makes a particular type of food seem more homely, unthreatening and 'normal' than if it sits on the supermarket shelf. A report published in 2004 by the major supermarket chain Sainsburys indicated that while sales of 'traditional British' dishes such as shepherd's pie and chicken casserole are in terminal decline, there seems to be an undimmed appetite among consumers of all classes for meals that are (or are presented as) Indian and Chinese in origin, with Mexican food coming in close behind. Indian- and Chinese-style meals were particularly popular with the under-16 age group, indicating that the tastes of the adults of the future are being profoundly shaped by food that is not 'traditional British' in style. The report concluded that by the year 2034, it was unlikely that more than one out of four meals eaten in Britain would involve 'traditionally British' dishes like steak and kidney pie or sausages and mash. Instead, the supermarket's researchers concluded that flavours and ingredients from as far afield as Japan, North Africa and Peru would by that time have become familiar parts of the British culinary scene (Sayid, 2004).

In the second case, we can identify the *creolization of cuisine*, a process in which both ingredients and styles of preparation from different places are melded together to create something novel. As we saw above, there is nothing particularly new about this. What we take as 'national' food cultures often involve ingredients that have come from very far away indeed – Italy and the tomato being a particularly striking case in point. What has happened over the last thirty years or so is an acceleration and a deepening of processes towards different culinary 'traditions' (most of which were always 'hybrid' in one way or another anyway) meeting and mixing with each other, sometimes at the express intention of chefs and others involved in culinary affairs, sometimes less so. One might expect that when a particular dish is made in a country in which it did not originate, it would undergo certain transformations – not only might the ingredients be slightly different in its new context, but also preparation techniques and culinary expectations might be divergent too. One would be hard pressed to find in the Indian subcontinent a dish corresponding very closely to what is sold in Britain as 'curry'. The latter is a 'creole' dish in that it has melded certain subcontinental spices and preparation techniques with the British taste for substantial amounts of meat in a rich gravy. It is not too much of an exaggeration to regard the curry as a sort of 'traditional' British beef (or chicken, or lamb, or whatever) stew with an 'Indian' accent.

At the more elevated level of the world of high-level chefs, creolization processes have become very important indeed in some ways over the last decade or so. In this area, *fusion cuisine* has become a recognized new genre, with its own celebrity chefs, restaurants and cookbooks. If one goes to a major city that borders the Pacific Ocean, such as San Francisco or Sydney, one encounters a large number of restaurants specializing in 'Pacific Rim' cuisine. This is a form of cooking that draws upon and blends a series of different culinary influences from across the Pacific area. One might encounter, for example, single dishes that contain ingredients and methods of preparation taken from the 'traditional' culinary cultures of Japan, China and Bali. Sometimes this just involves a relatively crude mixing and matching of different traditions – just adding lemongrass and coconut milk, two of the staples of South-East Asian cuisines, to everything is how those sceptical of such experimentation might describe these efforts. But more thoughtful and sophisticated forms of fusion cookery are also possible. On one memorable occasion in Sydney, I dined on emu lasagne at a restaurant oriented around fusing 'international' cooking methods with the spice repertoire of Australian aboriginal food culture. The combination of Italian-style preparation with unfamiliar, indigenous Australian flavourings such as the barks of trees that grow in the outback, was an instance of contemporary global cultural commingling presented on one plate.

There seems today to be almost boundless scope for taking different food traditions, spiking them with new flavours and ideas, and then looking to see what the results are like. One increasingly need not live anywhere near the Pacific to try this sort of experimental food. The literally named chain of restaurants *Asia de Cuba* has branches in locales as removed from the environs of the Pacific as New York and London.

What they offer are dishes that draw upon the cookery traditions of both East Asia and the Caribbean island of Cuba. By drawing on the latter, the *Asia de Cuba* chefs are themselves drawing on a historically earlier type of 'fusion' cuisine, in that the cuisine of Cuba contains strong African and European influences. What diners are eating in such restaurants, therefore, is just the most up-to-date version of culinary blending and mixing processes that have been going on for a long time, not just around the Pacific but across the Atlantic too. If self-conscious fusion experiments in food are primarily contemporary to our age, they draw upon earlier culinary fusions, caused by the ebb and flows of empire, travel and trade.

The third aspect of food practices that characterize our eating habits today that we will mention concerns what we can identify as the *connoisseurship of national cuisines*. Side by side with developments towards novel combinations of ingredients and flavours, there are also counter-trends towards defining and defending the parameters of particular 'national' and 'regional' cuisines. In these cases, certain interested parties claim to have found the essence of a particular cuisine, be it associated with a nation, a region, or a particular ethnic or other sort of group. A whole sub-field of the publishing industry has sprung up to cater for this market, selling cookbooks that claim to present the 'real Andalusia' or the 'true taste of Provence'. Here we have a concerted effort not only to capture the 'essence' of each particular cuisine but also to police what are acceptable or unacceptable versions of particular dishes. Today we have a whole series of culinary entrepreneurs – cookbook authors, food journalists, TV food programme hosts, and so on – all concerned to dictate what is 'authentic' in a cuisine and what is not.

What this sort of rule-making conveniently forgets is that many of the cuisines that have apparently been around untouched since the mists of time are themselves hybrids, cobbled together as the result of migrations and trade. Up until relatively recently, no one needed to bother with the 'purity' or otherwise of a cuisine, because changes to a cuisine tended to happen relatively slowly and incrementally, and thus as it were 'organically', over time. But now with new fusions and combinations being created, both consciously and less consciously, all the time at an often dizzying speed, there seems to some more and more need to draw demarcation lines around 'true' expressions of a food culture, and to identify and condemn mere ersatz imitations of them and bizarre fusion deviations from the norm. For pizza purists, one should not put pineapple on top of one's pizza, as if to do so were a great crime against Italian civilization; but the ubiquitous tomato topping on the pizza itself hardly counts as very 'traditional', if by the latter we mean what Italians ate more than a few centuries ago.

Here we have an instance of deliberate and self-conscious attempts at cultural 'localization', a process not confined to the realm of food. As 'global' fusions and hybrids seem to spin out of control, for some people it seems necessary to reclaim essentially 'local' virtues, in this case ingredients, recipes and flavours. As Manuel Castells (1997: 2) argues, as people in different parts of the world feel threatened by 'globalization' – involving the loss of economic security, national self-determination and cultural traditions – they turn towards 'expressions of collective identity that challenge globalization ... on behalf of cultural singularity and people's control over their lives and environment'. Far from destroying more local and specific senses of belonging, identity and affiliation, globalization processes may actually help reinvigorate these.

But the *reclaiming* of the local as often as not involves actually *reinventing* it, as the example of food illustrates. One might, for example, think that artisanally produced (i.e. non-mass production) pasta is a key part of ancient southern Italian food culture. But pasta only became widespread in the region in the eighteenth century, hardly a period long enough away from our own to count as 'ancient'. It would seem, then, that as with so much else on a globalizing planet, 'authenticity' in food is more a comforting myth in a world of ever-changing food fashions and fads than a secure basis for grounding one's identity. Yet as long as the complex history of food migrations and transplantations throughout history, and especially the last 500 years, is kept from one's mind, one may remain relatively comfortable in the everyday belief that types of food and particular places are unproblematically and securely connected. Whether further developments in fusion cuisine, and the ever greater appetite for 'foreign' dishes in Western countries, dim that belief remains to be seen.

CONCLUSION: COSMOPOLITAN FUTURES?

In this chapter I have examined the various ways in which we could see the cultural forces which shape everyday practices becoming more or

less homogenized, characterized either by 'global' uniformity and sameness through the power of an American-led 'global culture', or by cultural hybridity, difference and the reassertion of locality and specificity.
I think it is fairly clear that both such master trends are at work in
everyday life today, both influencing in complicated and often ambigu-
ous ways different aspects and levels of everyday activities, and to some
extent balancing each other out. We do not face a total condition of
local cultural wipe-out at the behest of global corporate and media culture, but neither are our everyday lives nirvanas of cultural openness,
eclecticism and celebrations of diversity, as some more optimistic
observers might have us believe.

The current cultural configuration of everyday life is an unsettled
– and constantly unsettling – *mélange* of the globally same and the
locally diverse, with the latter continuing to exist in the face of the
former, and the former in some ways stimulating both old and new
versions of the latter. For a person of my leftist political persuasions,
it would be nice to conclude that everyday life is becoming ever more
characterized by 'cosmopolitanism', a mindset made up of respect for
and interest in the cultures of 'others' and an open-minded sense of
cultural experimentation and a liking of fusions and hybrids
(Hannerz, 1990; Fine and Cohen, 2002). But liking different
'national' types of food and going to fusion cuisine restaurants is not
necessarily linked to actually doing something concrete about Third
World debt, global warming and a whole host of other problems that
are 'global' in scope. One can be a 'cosmopolitan' in one's cultural
tastes without being a 'cosmopolitan' in one's other activities, including political ones. Indeed, being seen to have cosmopolitan tastes can
be a way for those with high levels of cultural and other forms of capital to differentiate themselves from the 'common herd' who are seen
to be stuck within the confines of more local and parochial concerns
(Calhoun, 2002). Moreover, talk about cultural fusions and hybrids
and transnational flows should not blind us to the fact that, as
Michael Billig (1995) so brilliantly demonstrates, 'national' sentiments and feelings continue to be influential in everyday life,
whether through the means of newspaper reporting or just mundane
talk in which we identify ourselves as essentially 'British' or 'German'
or whatever. On the other hand, it is clear that the effects of what we
call 'globalization' on how we think and act are always going to be

diverse and somewhat unpredictable. The globalization of culture and everyday life is never going to involve foregone conclusions.

CONCLUSION

In a book about the often tacit assumptions that underpin everyday activities, it is rather appropriate to conclude by drawing attention to one of the assumptions that underpins one of any writer's (sort of) everyday activities, namely composing conclusions to books. In such contexts, one is often expected magisterially to review what one has said and then, on the basis of identifying the apparent failures of every other author in the field in grasping the subject matter to hand, to propose a grand programme that will set aright study of that field and take it in brilliant new directions.

I am always rather sceptical about such grand programmes, in major part because I often feel I can discern in them the faint aroma of old wine that has been decanted into newish bottles. The great problem with all big claims as to how things should be in the future is that the achievements of the past either get accidentally ignored or are deliberately forgotten. Given my reliance in this book on the ideas of a whole host of people, both dead and alive, I can hardly here claim single-handedly to have reinvented the wheel that is the sociology of culture and of everyday life. I am very conscious that greater talents than my own have tread on this ground before me, and I am greatly in their debt.

In particular, when rereading for this book some of Georg Simmel's work that I had not read for a long time, I was very much struck by how brilliantly insightful his work continues to be, even when the context in which he produced his insights is in some ways – but of course not all ways – long gone. Although he is open to justified criticism on the grounds that his views on cultural matters were formulated from the viewpoint of the comfortable armchair rather than of the ethnographer pounding the streets of the city, leafing through his writings can often yield quite startling moments of recognition on behalf of the reader, or at least this one anyway. If anyone deserves to be elevated as the patron saint of the cultural sociology of everyday life – if he has not already been so – it is Simmel. Reading him reminds one that sociological comprehension, of everyday as well as of other matters, need not be decoupled from imagination and a creative response to the complexities of human life.

In saying that, I can feel bearing down upon me the tacit norms that apply as to the desirability of programmatic conclusions to books, so I will now turn to consider what I for one have learned from putting this book together. My reflections will consider how the cultural sociological (or sociology of culture, if you prefer) study of 'everyday affairs' should in the future progress, but it will deal with those in terms of a particular set of everyday affairs, namely how academics carry on their analytic business at the present time.

I am going to approach this issue at first autobiographically, as that helps to give a sense of the concrete problems involved here. As an undergraduate student, and for reasons I greatly suspect to do with the sort of educational institution I was attending, I was convinced of the greatness and nobility of what I liked to call 'theory' and the great and awful vulgarity of what I also liked to call 'empiricism', by which I meant empirical research of all hues. If a book or article engaged with the empirical level of human affairs, I rejected it as robustly as if I were a Protestant reformer faced with a text by Cardinal Bellarmine. As you might imagine, I was then a big fan of those who occupied the position of, as it were, the 'theorists' theorists', figures like Althusser and Adorno, those prone rather to *de haut en bas* pronouncements that would appal the 'empiricists' but would be lapped up by eager young would-be 'theorists' like myself.

That phase has passed, and has been buried finally by the writing of this book. Now, after writing three monographs and after full-time employment as a sociologist for almost a decade, I have managed to come down off my high-horse and see what silliness was involved in those sorts of attitudes, at least if they are taken to extremes, as I was indeed prone to take them. What I was unintentionally doing was reproducing in thought and opinion the division of labour that pertains in modern universities. As Durkheim remarked a hundred years ago, it is difficult in modern intellectual conditions to be a non-specialist, someone who roams across different areas and sorts of endeavour, finding out how to do diverse things like understand Heidegger *and* be familiar with statistical research methods. Either you cannot find the time and energy to be such a Renaissance person – the very name a reminder that the day of the all-rounder lies more in the past than the present – or you are ridiculed for being a dilettante and a jack-of-all-trades. What I was doing was valorizing one element of the intellectual division of labour in sociology and the social sciences more generally – the apparently more 'glamorous' bit that requires a certain form of cultural capital, a certain facility with philosophical terms and words (deliberately?) off-putting for the uninitiated. Concomitantly, I was derogating, as those who like to associate themselves with the 'theoretical' side of the social sciences sometimes like to do, the 'other' side, those who, as I saw it, soiled themselves with the daily grind of empirical data collection. I thought I was one of the fly-boys of the theorists' equivalent of the RAF, buzzing nonchalantly over the massed ranks of the 'poor bloody infantry' of empirical researchers.

I have now come down to earth, if not with a bump then with the realization that I was merely reproducing, in a very unhelpful way, the worst sides of a highly specialized division of academic labour. I don't think that it is facile to say that this organization of intellectual production can be very debilitating. Of course, complex activities need specialists to carry them out, and I am not now about to jump out of the closet parading my Maoist, anti-differentiationist credentials. But too much specialization is harmful to forms of social science which seek to involve more than just the 'brilliant' but empirically unproven thoughts of a few 'great thinkers' on the one hand, and the theoretically impoverished presentation of 'data' on the other. But everyday life in the contemporary academy tends to be structured around those two poles, with some people hovering at one end, doing their own specific things, and others lingering at the other, doing their own particular things too. There are occasional outbreaks of hostility between the two groups, which can be quite amusing in the way that sectarian struggles between highly dogmatic political factions has a certain black comedy about it. But for the most part, the mundane organization of academic activity in sociology and cognate areas generally tends to involve not even their talking past each other but not talking to each other at all. Do people who specialize in large-scale data sets publish in 'social theory' and 'cultural theory' journals? Do the people who publish in the latter sorts of places know what log-linear analysis is? (I don't, and I used not to care, but now I feel uneasy at this ignorance.)

This sort of situation is not helpful, I submit to you, because it means that social scientists are even more crippled than they need be in trying to capture the complexity of human experience, here meant in the widest sense of the term, to include both micro-level 'everyday' contexts, and more macro-level institutional and structural forms and forces. Over-specialization in either macro or micro analysis, too much of an orientation to either one of 'quantitative' or 'qualitative' methods, an excessive commitment to 'theory' or 'data collection' – none of these imbalances are helpful, precisely because they close down rather than open up the complexity of the phenomena they are examining. Certain things are seen and represented as if that was the whole story. But if your telescope is fixed at the moon, you might miss the small fact that there are other things in the sky too, and that they might be interesting.

This is a particularly acute problem for the study of the forms that everyday life takes in different social and cultural contexts. As I have said at various places throughout the book, everyday contexts are complex. This is because people are complex. Accounts we give of people in their everyday lives are inevitably hugely selective, grasping certain things and missing out whole swathes of other things. This problem is made even worse if your explicit focus is on 'culture' in everyday life. How do you capture the evanescent, the transitory and the fleeting, matters hidden from direct view, things you can sometimes only see out of the corner of your eye?

Even a multi-faceted and well-rounded form of social scientific investigation that embraced all of the antinomies noted above – theoretical sophistication *and* analytical rigour, qualitative *and* quantitative procedures, both micrological sensitivity *and* macrological breadth – would find it impossible to know *everything* there is to know about the cultural fabrics and textures of everyday existence. But a social science that did not at the very least seek to achieve a rounded and alert gaze – or rather, series of complementary gazes – would discover even less.

Time and again throughout the book it has been apparent that the debates on particular issues swing back and forth between more 'theoretical' pronouncements and more 'empirical' statements, often presented as rebuttals of the former. This can sometimes degenerate, or so it seems, into some kind of intellectuals' version of a pantomime – 'Oh yes it is!', 'Oh no it isn't!', 'Oh yes it is!' Time and again, we get big statements from 'theorists' like 'modernity is over', 'we're all postmodern now', 'art is a fraud', 'ordinary people are dim', 'globalization is making us all into baseball cap wearing, Coke drinking morons', and so on. Then we get the micro-level researchers' responses, which are almost always along the lines of 'but if you go to place X and locale Y, you'll see it's not at all like what the theories say'. Now, what the empirical researchers are saying can be incredibly valuable. They have at least made the effort to find out what is going on in certain specific lifeworlds (which is more than I, as a 'theorist', have ever done). But empirical work uninformed by the broader perspective that 'theory' can provide is as one-sided and as suspect as theory denuded of empirical justification.

In the same vein, claiming uncritically that 'ordinary people' are incredibly creative and 'resistive' is as silly as pontificating wildly from your ivory tower about the vulgarity of the plebs. Social science, if it has to have any claims to being more than just bias, cant and folk wisdom, must seek to look at both the macro-level structures of power and domination in societies *and* micro-level contexts that may be characterized by effervescence, turmoil and flux. But assuming beforehand that everything in mundane contexts either involves automatic reproduction of the power of the powerful or eternal joyful carnivals of lower-class 'resistance' is as silly as saying that you know how perfectly accurately to predict the future. The questions that we have looked at in this book – about power and resistance, globalization and localization, and so on – are only empirically answerable, but in turn the questions can only be framed and the data interpreted through specific theoretical lenses.

The problems of myopia attendant upon an academy carved up into separate, and too often discreetly sealed-off, areas applies not just within sociology and the social sciences but also between the latter and the natural sciences. Far, far too often these talk past each other, when they are not spitting viciously at each other like angry cats, caricaturing each other like crazy. A natural science perspective on a certain issue can see certain aspects of it, but not others, but there can be a tendency to regard what can be seen as the only aspect of that thing and therefore its 'essence'. Given that the social sciences, particularly under the influence (pun intended) of post-structuralism and post-modernism, are so suspicious of 'essences', especially the ones that biologists and evolutionary psychologists like to talk about, it is highly ironic that they too see certain aspects of a phenomenon but then misrecognize the aspects of it that they can discern, as its very essence.

Here we come up against the problem I flagged up at the start of this book. Certain branches of the social sciences have in recent years come more and more to assert that 'biology' is irrelevant to human life as the latter is 'cultural' through and through. It is asserted that, for example, it is not just gender that is a cultural construction but actually 'sex' too – there is no such thing as 'biology', biological drives and suchlike, they are all just a matter of culture. What this and other assertions like it utterly fail to recognize is that if you have an analytical framework that can only discern the cultural aspects of human life, then that is all you will see. What you will *not* see is precisely what those equipped with other frameworks can, in this case that there are certain ways in which biology plays a profound role – as, indeed, does 'culture' – in how human beings think and act. In Chapter 1 I tried to be very careful in my choice of language – I believe it indeed to be the case that human beings are not *wholly* determined by biological structures and drives (no sensible natural scientist does either). We are indeed 'cultural' beings (as are the great apes to a certain extent). But to claim that the human body is a purely cultural phenomenon, and that everyday life is wholly unaffected by people's biological characteristics, is to indulge in a dogma so harmful to progressing understanding of human life that it hardly bears thinking about – and this from 'deconstructionists' who like to challenge (other people's) dogmas!

I will end, however, on a more positive note. To paraphrase Matthew Arnold, I believe that the great help out of our present difficulties is not 'Culture' with a big 'c' or even with a small 'c', but a reflexive – that is to say, self-critical – awareness of the problems wrought by a highly specialized intellectual division of labour, the forms of blindness it brings in its wake, and the dogmatic retrenchment of special interests that it encourages. It is when a culture of fully rounded social scientific practice comes to characterize our daily endeavours that we will be able to see more clearly the subtleties, paradoxes and ambiguities of culture and everyday life themselves.

BIBLIOGRAPHY

Adam, B. (1994) *Time and Social Theory*, Cambridge: Polity.

Adorno, T. W. (1967) 'Perennial Fashion – Jazz', in *Prisms*, London: Neville Spearman.

Adorno, T. W. and Horkheimer, M. (1992 [1944]) *Dialectic of Enlightenment*, London: Verso.

Albrecht, M. C. (1970) 'Art as an Institution', in Milton C. Albrecht, J. H. Barnett and M. Griff (eds) *The Sociology of Art and Literature*, London: Gerald Duckworth, pp. 1–28.

Albrow, M. (1996) *The Global Age*, Cambridge: Polity.

Alexander, J. C. (1983) *Theoretical Logic in Sociology, Vol. III. The Classical Attempt At Theoretical Synthesis: Max Weber*, London: Routledge.

Ang, I (1995) *Living Room Wars: Rethinking Media Audiences for a Postmodern World*, London: Routledge.

Arnold, M. (1995 [1869]) 'Culture and Anarchy', in Stefan Collini (ed.) *Culture and Anarchy and Other Writings*, Cambridge: Cambridge University Press.

Augé, M. (1995) *Non-places: introduction to an anthropology of super-modernity*, London: Verso.

Axford, B (1995) *The Global System*, Cambridge: Polity.

Bakhtin, M. (1984) *Rabelais and His World*, Bloomington: Indiana University Press.

Barber, B. (1992) 'Jihad Vs. McWorld', *The Atlantic Monthly*, Vol. 269, No. 3, pp. 53–65.

Barthes, R. (1985) *The Fashion System*, London: Jonathan Cape.

—— (1993) *Mythologies*, London: Vintage.

Baudriallard, J. (1994 [1986]) *America*, trans. Chris Turner, London: Verso.

Bauman, Z. (1998) *Globalization: the human consequences*, Cambridge: Polity.

Beck, U. (1992) *Risk Society: towards a new modernity*, London: Sage.

—— (2000) *What Is Globalization?*, Cambridge: Polity.

Becker, H. (1974) 'Art as Collective Action', *American Sociological Review*, Vol. 39, No. 6, pp. 767–776.

—— (1984) *Art Worlds*, Berkeley: University of California Press.

Behan, B. (1990 [1958]) *Borstal Boy*, London: Arrow.

Berger, P. L. and Luckmann, T. (1967) *The Social Construction of Reality*, New York: Anchor.

Berman, M. (1983) *All That Is Solid Melts Into Air*, London: Verso.

Beynon, H. (1973) *Working for Ford*, London: Allen Lane.

Bhabha, H. (1994) *The Place of Culture*, London: Routledge.

Billig, M. (1995) *Banal Nationalism*, London: Sage.

Bosquet, M. [Andre Gorz] (1977 [1973]) *Capitalism in Crisis and Everyday Life*, trans. John Howe, Hassocks, Sussex: Harvester Press.

Bourdieu, P. (1990) *In Other Words*, Cambridge: Polity.

—— (1991) *Language and Symbolic Power*, Cambridge: Polity.

—— (1992) *Distinction: a social critique of the judgement of taste*, London: Routledge.

—— (1993) 'How Can One Be a Sports Fan?', in Simon During (ed.) *The Cultural Studies Reader*, London: Routledge.

—— (1998) *The State Nobility*, Cambridge: Polity.

Bourdieu, P. and Darbel, A. (1991) *The Love of Art*, Cambridge: Polity.

Bourdieu, P. and Passeron, J.-C. (1990) *Reproduction in Education, Society and Culture*, London: Sage.

Bove, J. *et al.* (2002) *The World Is Not For Sale: Farmers Against Junk Food*, London: Verso.

Brohm, J.-M. (1989) *Sport: A Prison or Measured Time*, London: Pluto Press.

Bryman, A. (2001) *Social Research Methods*, Oxford: Oxford University Press.

Budgeon, S. (2003) *Choosing A Self: Young Women and the Individualisation of Identity*, Westport, CT: Praeger.

Calhoun, C. (2002) 'The Class Consciousness of Frequent Travellers: Towards A Critique of Actually Existing Cosmopolitanism', in Steven Vertovec and Robin Cohen (eds) *Conceiving Cosmopolitanism: Theory, Context, and Practice*, Oxford: Oxford University Press, pp. 86–119.

Castells, M. (1997) *The Power of Identity, The Information Age: Economy, Society and* Culture, Vol. 2. Oxford: Blackwell.

Classen, C. (1996) 'Sugar Cane, Coca-Cola and Hypermarkets: Consumption and Surrealism in the Argentine North-West', in D. Howes (ed.) *Cross-Cultural Consumption: Global Markets, Local Realities*, London: Routledge, pp. 39–54.

Collins, R. (1986) *Max Weber: a skeleton key*, London: Sage.

Cvetkovich, A. and Kellner, D. (1997) 'Thinking Global and Local', in A. Cvetkovich and D. Kellner (eds) *Articulating the Global and the Local*, Boulder, CO: Westview.

Danto, A. C. (1974) 'The Transfiguration of the Commonplace', *Aesthetics and Art Criticism*, No. 33, pp. 139–148.

De Beauvoir, S. (1972 [1949]) *The Second Sex*, Harmondsworth: Penguin.

de Certeau, M. (1984) *The Practice of Everyday Life*, Vol. I, Berkeley: University of California Press.

—— (1997) *Culture in the Plural*, Minneapolis: University of Minnesota Press.

de Waal, F. (2002) *The Ape and the Sushi Master*, Harmondsworth: Penguin.

DiMaggio, P. (1986) 'Cultural Entrepreneurship in Nineteenth Century Boston: the creation of an organisational base for high culture in America', in R. Collins *et al.* (eds) *Media, Culture and Society: a critical reader*, London: Sage.

Durkheim, E. (1984 [1893]) *The Division of Labour in Society*, Basingstoke: Macmillan.

—— (2001 [1912]) *The Elementary Forms of the Religious Life*, Oxford: Oxford University Press.

Durkheim, E. and Mauss, M. (1969 [1903]) *Primitive Classification*, London: Cohen and West.

Eco, U. (1985) 'Reflections on The Name Of The Rose', *Encounter*, Vol. LXIV, April, pp. 7–19.

Eichberg, H. (1998) *Body Cultures: Essays on Sport, Space and Identity*, London: Routledge.

Elias, N. (1995) *Mozart: portrait of a genius*, Cambridge: Polity.

Etcoff, N. (2000) *Survival of the Prettiest: The Science of Beauty*, London: Abacus.

Fallows, J. (1996) 'Throwing Like a Girl', *Atlantic Monthly*, August. Online. Available:
<http://www.theatlantic.com/issues/96aug/throw/throw.htm>

Feifer, M. (1985) *Going Places*, Basingstoke: Macmillan.

Fernandez-Armesto, F. (2001) *Food: A History*, Basingstoke: Macmillan.

Fine, R. and Cohen, R. (2002) 'Four Cosmopolitan Moments', in Steven Vertovec and Robin Cohen (eds) *Conceiving Cosmopolitanism: Theory, Context, and Practice*, Oxford: Oxford University Press, pp. 137–164.

Fiske, J. (1987) *Television Culture*, London: Methuen.

—— (1989a) *Reading the Popular*, Boston: Unwin Hyman.

—— (1989b) *Understanding Popular Culture*, Boston: Unwin Hyman.

Foucault, M. (1981) *The History of Sexuality*, Vol. I, Harmondsworth: Penguin.

Freud, S. (1957) *Civilization and its Discontents*, London: Hogarth Press.

Friedman, T. (1999) *The Lexus and the Olive Tree*, London: HarperCollins.

Frisby, D. (1985) *Fragments of Modernity*, Cambridge: Polity.

—— (1990) *The Consequences of Modernity*, Cambridge: Polity.

—— (1991) *Modernity and Self-Identity*, Cambridge: Polity.

Frow, J. (1987) 'Accounting for Tastes: some problems in Bourdieu's sociology of culture', *Cultural Studies*, Vol. 1, No. 1, pp. 59–73.

Fukuyama, F. (1992) *The End of History and the Last Man*, London: Hamish Hamilton.

Garcia-Canclini, N. (1995) *Hybrid Cultures: Strategies for Entering and Leaving Modernity*, Minneapolis: University of Minnesota Press.

Giddens, A. (1990) *The Consequences of Modernity*, Cambridge: Polity.

—— (1991) *Modernity and Self-Identity*, Cambridge: Polity.

Gilloch, G. (1997) *Myth and Metropolis: Walter Benjamin and the City*, Cambridge: Polity.

Gimpel, J. (1969) *The Cult of Art: against art and artists*, London: Weidenfeld and Nicolson.

Giulianotti, R. (1999) *Football: A Sociology of the Global Game*, Cambridge: Polity.

Gouldner, A. (1975) 'Sociology and the Everyday Life', in Lewis A. Coser (ed.) *The Idea of Social Structure: Papers in Honor of Robert K. Merton*, New York: Harcourt Brace Jovanovich, pp. 417–432.

Gramsci, A. (1971) *Selections From the Prison Notebooks*, London: Lawrence and Wishart.

Greenberg, C. (1986 [1939]) 'Avant-garde and Kitsch', in John O'Brian (ed.) *Clement Greenberg: the collected essays and criticism, Vol. I, Perceptions and Judgments 1939–1944*, Chicago: University of Chicago Press.

Habermas, J. (1984) *The Theory of Communicative Action*, Vol. I, London: Heinemann.

—— (1987) *The Theory of Communicative Action*, Vol. I, Cambridge: Polity.

Hall, S. (1981) 'Cultural Studies: Two Paradigms', in T. Bennett, G. Martin, C. Mercer and J. Woollacott (eds) *Culture, Ideology and Social Process: a Reader*, London: Open University Press, pp. 19–37.

Hall, S. and Whannell, P. (1964) *The Popular Arts*, London: Heinemann.

Hannerz, U. (1989) 'Notes on the Global Ecumene', *Public Culture*, Vol. 1, No. 2, pp. 66–75.

—— (1990) 'Cosmopolitans and Locals in World Culture', in Mike Featherstone *et al.* (eds) *Global Culture*, London: Sage.

—— (1996) *Transnational Connections: Culture, People, Places*, London: Routledge.

Hardt, M. and Negri, A. (2000) *Empire*, Cambridge, MA: Harvard University Press.

Harris, D. (1992) *From Class Struggle to the Politics of Pleasure: the effects of Gramscianism on cultural studies*, London: Routledge.

Hassan, I. (1985) 'The Culture of Postmodernism', *Theory, Culture and Society*, Vol. 2, No. 3.

Hebdige, D. (1979) *Subculture: The Meaning of Style*, London: Routledge.

Held, D. and McGrew, A. (2000) *The Global Transformations Reader: An Introduction to the Globalization Debate*, Cambridge: Polity.

Held, D. *et al.* (eds) (1999) *Global Transformations: Politics, Economics and Culture*, Cambridge: Polity.

Hobsbawm, E. and Ranger, T. (1983) *The Invention of Tradition*, Cambridge: Cambridge University Press.

Hochschild, A. R. (2003) *The Managed Heart: Commercialisation of Human Feeling*, Los Angeles: University of California Press.

Hoggart, R. (1962 [1957]) *The Uses of Literacy: aspects of working-class life with special reference to publications and entertainment*, Harmondsworth: Penguin.

—— (1970) 'Literature and Society', in *Speaking to Each Other, Volume II, About Literature*, Harmondsworth: Penguin.

—— (1982) 'Humanistic Studies and Mass Culture', in *An English Temper: essays on education, culture, and communications*, London: Chatto and Windus.

—— (1996) *The Way We Live Now*, London: Pimlico.

Horkheimer, M. (1972) 'Art and Mass Culture', in *Critical Theory: selected essays*, New York: Herder and Herder.

Howes, D. (1996) 'Commodities and Cultural Borders', in D. Howes (ed.) *Cross-Cultural Consumption: Global Markets, Local Realities*, London: Routledge, pp. 1–18.

Huntington, S. (1998) *The Clash of Civilizations and the Remaking of World Order*, London: Simon and Schuster.

Husserl, E. (1970) *The Crisis of European Sciences and Transcendental Phenomenology*, trans. David Carr, Evanston, IL: Northwestern University Press.

Inglis, D. (2001) *A Sociological History of Excretory Experience: Defecatory Manners and Toiletry Technologies*, Lewiston, NY: Mellen.

Inglis, D. and Holmes, M. (2002) 'Highland Haunts: Scottish spectres and the spatial politics of tourism', *Annals of Tourism Research*, Vol. 30, No. 1.

Inglis, D. and Hughson, J. (2003) *Confronting Culture: Sociological Vistas*, Cambridge: Polity.

James, A. (1996) 'Cooking the Books: Global or Local Identities in Contemporary British Food Cultures?', in D. Howes (ed.) *Cross-Cultural Consumption: Global Markets, Local Realities*, London: Routledge, pp 77–93.

Jameson, F. (1992) *Postmodernism: or, the Cultural Logic of Late Capitalism*, London: Verso.

Kadushin, C. (1976) 'Networks and Circles in the Production of Culture', in Richard A. Peterson (ed.) *The Production of Culture*, Beverly Hills, CA: Sage.

Katz, E. and Liebes, T. (1985) 'Mutual Aid in the Decoding of Dallas', in P. Drummond and R. Paterson (eds) *Television in Transition*, London: British Film Institute.

Klein, N. (2001) *No Logo*, London: Flamingo.

Kroeber, A. (1945) 'The Ancient Oikoumene as an Historic Culture Aggregate', *Journal of the Royal Anthropological Institute of Great Britain and Ireland*, Vol. 75, No. 1/2, pp. 9–20.

—— (1948) *Anthropology: Race, Language, Culture, Psychology, Prehistory*, New York: Harcourt, Brace & World.

Kroeber, A. L. and Kluckhohn, C. (1963 [1952]) *Culture: a critical review of concepts and definitions*, New York, Random House.

Lasch, C. (1991) *The Culture of Narcissism*, New York: Norton.

Leavis, F. R. (1993 [1948]) *The Great Tradition*, Harmondsworth: Penguin.

Lefebvre, H. (1971 [1968]) *Everyday Life in the Modern World*, trans. Sacha Rabinovitch, London: Allen Lane.

—— (1993 [1974]) *The Production of Space*, trans. Donald Nicholson-Smith, Oxford: Blackwell.

Lowenthal, L. (1957) *Literature, Popular Culture and Society*, Englewood Cliffs, NJ: Prentice Hall.

Lynd, R. S. and Lynd, H. M. (1957 [1929]) *Middletown: a study in modern American culture*, New York: Harcourt Brace.

Lyotard, J.-F. (1984) *The Postmodern Condition: a report on the condition of knowledge*, Manchester: Manchester University Press.

MacCannell, D. (1974) 'Staged Authenticity: arrangements of social space in tourist settings', *American Journal of Sociology*, Vol. 79, No. 3.

Macdonald, D. (1978 [1953]) 'A Theory of Mass Culture', in Peter Davison *et al.* (eds) *Literary Taste, Culture, and Mass Communication*, Vol. I, Teaneck, NJ: Chadwyck-Healey.

Macdonald, K. M. (1995) *The Sociology of the Professions*, London: Sage.

Mannheim, K. (1956) *Essays on the Sociology of Culture*, London: Routledge.

Marx, K. (1983 [1848]) 'Manifesto of the Communist Party', in Eugene Kamenka (ed.) *The Portable Karl Marx*, Harmondsworth: Penguin.

Mattelart, A. (2000) *Networking the World, 1794–2000*, Minneapolis: University of Minnesota Press.

Mauss, M. (1979) *Sociology and Psychology: Essays*, London: Routledge.

McGuigan, J. (1992) *Cultural Populism*, London: Routledge.

McLellan, D. (1984) *The Thought of Karl Marx*, Basingstoke: Macmillan.

Mead, G. H. (1938) *Philosophy of the Act*, Chicago: University of Chicago Press.

Meethan, K. (2001) *Tourism in Global Society: Place, Culture, Consumption*, Basingstoke: Palgrave.

Merton, R. K. (1976) *Sociological Ambivalence and Other Essays*, New York: Free Press.

Miller, D. (1992) 'The Young and Restless in Trinidad: a case of the local and global in mass consumption', in R. Silverstone and E. Hirsch (eds) *Consuming Technology*, London: Routledge.

Morley, D. (1980) *The 'Nationwide' Audience: structure and decoding*, London: British Film Institute.

—— (1981) 'Interpreting Television', in *Popular Culture and Everyday Life* (Block 3 of U203 *Popular Culture*), Milton Keynes: Open University Press, pp. 40–68.

Mozart, W. A. (2000) 'Letter to His Father in Salzburg, April 11, 1781', in Robert Spaethling (ed.) *Mozart's Letters, Mozart's Life*, London: Faber and Faber.

Orwell, G. (2003 [1933]) *Down and out in Paris and London*, Harmondsworth: Penguin.

Parsons, T. (1961) 'Introduction – Part Four – Culture and the Social System', in Talcott Parsons *et al.* (eds) *Theories of Society*, Vol. II, Glencoe, NY: Free Press.

Pepys, S. (2003) *The Diary of Samuel Pepys – A Selection*, ed. Robert Latham, Harmondsworth: Penguin.

Perec, G. (1997 [1974]) 'Species of Spaces', in *Species of Spaces and Other Pieces*, trans. John Sturrock, London: Penguin.

Peterson, R. A. (1972) 'A Process Model of the Folk, Popular, and Fine Art Phases of Jazz', in C. Nanry (ed.) *American Music: from Storyville to Woodstock*, New Brunswick, NJ: Rutgers University Press.

Peterson, R. A. and Kern, R. M. (1996) 'Changing Highbrow Taste: from snob to omnivore', *American Sociological Review*, Vol. 61, No.5, pp. 900–907.

Pieterse, J. N. (1995) 'Globalization as Hybridization', in M. Featherstone *et al.* (eds) *Global Modernities*, London: Sage.

Plummer, K. (2001) *Documents of Life 2: An Invitation to Critical Humanism*, London: Sage.

Reynolds, N. (2004) '"Shocking" Urinal Better Than Picasso Because They Say So', *Daily Telegraph*, 2 December, p. 5.

Riesman, D. (1950) *The Lonely Crowd*, Mew Haven, CT: Yale University Press.

Ritzer, G. (1992) *The McDonaldization of Society: an investigation into the changing character of contemporary social life*, Thousands Oaks, CA: Pine Forge.

Robertson, R. (1992) *Globalization: social theory and global culture*, London: Sage.

Robertson, R. and Inglis, D. (2004) 'The Global *Animus*: in the tracks of world-consciousness', *Globalizations*, Vol. 1, No. 1, pp. 38–49.

Sassen, S. (1998) *Globalization and Its Discontents*, New York: Free Press.

Saussure, F. (1959 [1906–1911]) *Course in General Linguistics*, ed. Charles Bally and Albert Sechehaye, New York: Philosophical Library.

Sayid, R. (2004) 'Will Traditional British Grub Soon Be A Thing of the Pasta?', *Daily Mirror*, October 29, p. 38.

Scruton, R. (1998) *An Intelligent Person's Guide To Modern Culture*, London: Duckworth.

Seneca (1889) 'Consolatio Ad Helvia/Addressed to His Mother Helvia: Of Consolation', in *L. Annaeus Seneca: minor dialogues*, trans. Aubrey Stewart, London: George Bell and Sons.

Shils, E. (1978 [1961]) 'Mass Society and Its Culture', in Peter Davison *et al.* (eds) *Literary Taste, Culture, and Mass Communication*, Vol. I, Teaneck, NJ: Chadwyck-Healey.

Shiner, L. (2001) *The Invention of Art: a cultural history*, Chicago: Chicago University Press.

Shrum, W. (1991) 'Critics and Publics: cultural mediation in highbrow and popular performing arts', *American Journal of Sociology*, Vol. 97, No. 2, pp. 347–375.

Simmel, G. (1950) 'Metropolis and Mental Life', in Kurt H. Wolff (trans. and ed.) *The Sociology of Georg Simmel*, New York: Free Press.

—— (1990 [1907]) *The Philosophy of Money*, ed. David Frisby, Tom Bottomore and David Frisby (trans.), London: Routledge.

—— (1997) 'The Problem of Style', in David Frisby and Mike Featherstone (eds) *Simmel On Culture: Selected Writings*, London: Sage, pp. 211–217.

Sklair, L. (2004) *Globalization: Capitalism and Its Alternatives*, Oxford: Oxford University Press.

Smith, S. (2001) *Misadventures*, Edinburgh: Canongate.

Stacey, J. (1994) *Stargazing: Hollywood and Female Spectatorship*, London: Routledge.

Stallabrass, J. (1996) *Gargantua: manufactured mass culture*, London: Verso.

Stallybrass, P. and White, A. (1986) *The Politics and Poetics of Transgression*, London: Methuen.

Steinbeck, J. (2003) *Of Men and Their Making*, Harmondsworth: Penguin.

Strauss, A. (1970) 'The Art School and Its Students: A study and An Interpretation', in Milton C. Albrecht, James H. Barnett and Mason Griff (eds) *The Sociology of Art and Literature: a reader*, London: Gerald Duckworth.

Sumner, W. G. (1961 [1906]) 'On the Mores', in Talcott Parsons *et al.* (eds) *Theories of Society*, Vol. II, Glencoe, NY: Free Press.

Thompson, E. P. (1967) 'Time, Work-Discipline and Industrial Capitalism', *Past and Present*, Vol. 36, pp. 57–97.

Thompson, J. B. (1995) *The Media and Modernity: A Social Theory of the Media*, Cambridge: Polity.

Tomlinson, J. (1997) *Cultural Imperialism: A Critical Introduction*, London: Pinter.

Truzzi, M. (1968) *Sociology and Everyday Life*, Englewood Cliffs, NJ: Prentice Hall.

Tunstall, J. (1977) *The Media Are American*, London: Constable.

Turner, B. (1996) *For Weber: essays on the sociology of fate*, London: Sage.

Twitchell, J. (1992) *Carnival Culture: the trashing of taste in America*, New York: Columbia University Press.

Urry, J. (2000) 'Mobile Sociology', *British Journal of Sociology*, Vol. 51, No. 1, pp. 185–203.

—— (2001) *The Tourist Gaze: leisure and travel in contemporary societies*, 2nd edition, London: Sage.

—— (2004) 'The "System" of Automobility', *Theory, Culture and Society*, Vol. 21, No. 4/5, October, pp. 25–40.

Van Gogh, V. (2004 [1884]) 'Letter From Vincent Van Gogh to Theo Van Gogh, Nuenen, October 1884'. Online. Available: <http://webexhibits.org/vangogh/letter/14/381.htm?qp=business.sales> (accessed 18 December 2004).

Veblen, T. (1994 [1899]) *The Theory of the Leisure Class*, New York: Dover.

Virilio, P. (1986) *Speed and Politics: An Essay on Dromology*, trans. Mark Polizzotti, New York: Semiotext(e).

Walby, S. (1990) *Theorizing Patriarchy*, Oxford: Blackwell.

Waters, M. (1995) *Globalization*, London: Routledge.

Weber, M. (1930) *The Protestant Ethic and the Spirit of Capitalism*, London: Methuen.

—— (1958) *The Rational and Social Foundations of Music*, Carbondale, IL: Southern Illinois University Press.

—— (1978) 'The Nature of Social Action', in W. G. Runciman (ed.) *Weber: Selections In Translation*, Cambridge: Cambridge University Press.

Werbner, P. (1997) 'Introduction: the dialectics of cultural hybridity', in Pnina Werbner and Tariq Modood (eds) *Debating Cultural Hybridity: multi-cultural identities and the politics of anti-racism*, London: Zed.

Williams, R. (1958) *Culture and Society 1780–1950*, London: Chatto and Windus.

—— (1976) *Keywords: a vocabulary of culture and society*, Glasgow: Fontana.

—— (1980 [1961]) *The Long Revolution*, Harmondsworth: Penguin.

—— (1981) *Culture*, Glasgow: Fontana.

—— (1989 [1958]) 'Culture is Ordinary', in R. Williams, *Resources of Hope: Culture, Democracy, Socialism*, London: Verso.

Willis, P. (1977) *Learning to Labour: How Working Class Kids get Working Class Jobs*, Aldershot: Gower.

—— (1990) *Common Culture: Symbolic Work at Play in the Cultural Activities of Young People*, Milton Keynes: Open University Press.

Young, I. M. (1990) 'Throwing Like A Girl: a phenomenology of feminine body comportment, motility and spatiality', in Iris Marion Young, *Throwing Like A Girl and Other Essays in Feminist Philosophy and Social Theory*, Bloomington: Indiana University Press.

Zolberg, V. (1992) 'Barrier or Leveller? The case of the art museum', in Michele Lamont and Marcel Fournier (eds) *Cultivating Differences: symbolic boundaries and the making of inequality*, Chicago: University of Chicago Press, pp. 187–209.

INDEX